BE the BANK!

BE the BANK!

How the Wealthy **CONTROL AND COMPOUND** Their Money and How You Can Too!

DARREN MITCHELL

Redwood Publishing, LLC
Orange County, California

Printed in the United States of America and Canada
First Printing, 2020

Published by:
Redwood Publishing, LLC
Orange County, California
info@redwooddigitalpublishing.com
www.redwooddigitalpublishing.com

ISBN: 978-1-952106-40-8 (paperback)
ISBN: 978-1-952106-41-5 (ebook)

Library of Congress Control Number: 2020908040

Interior Design: Ghislain Viau
Cover Design: Michelle Manley

10 9 8 7 6 5 4 3 2 1

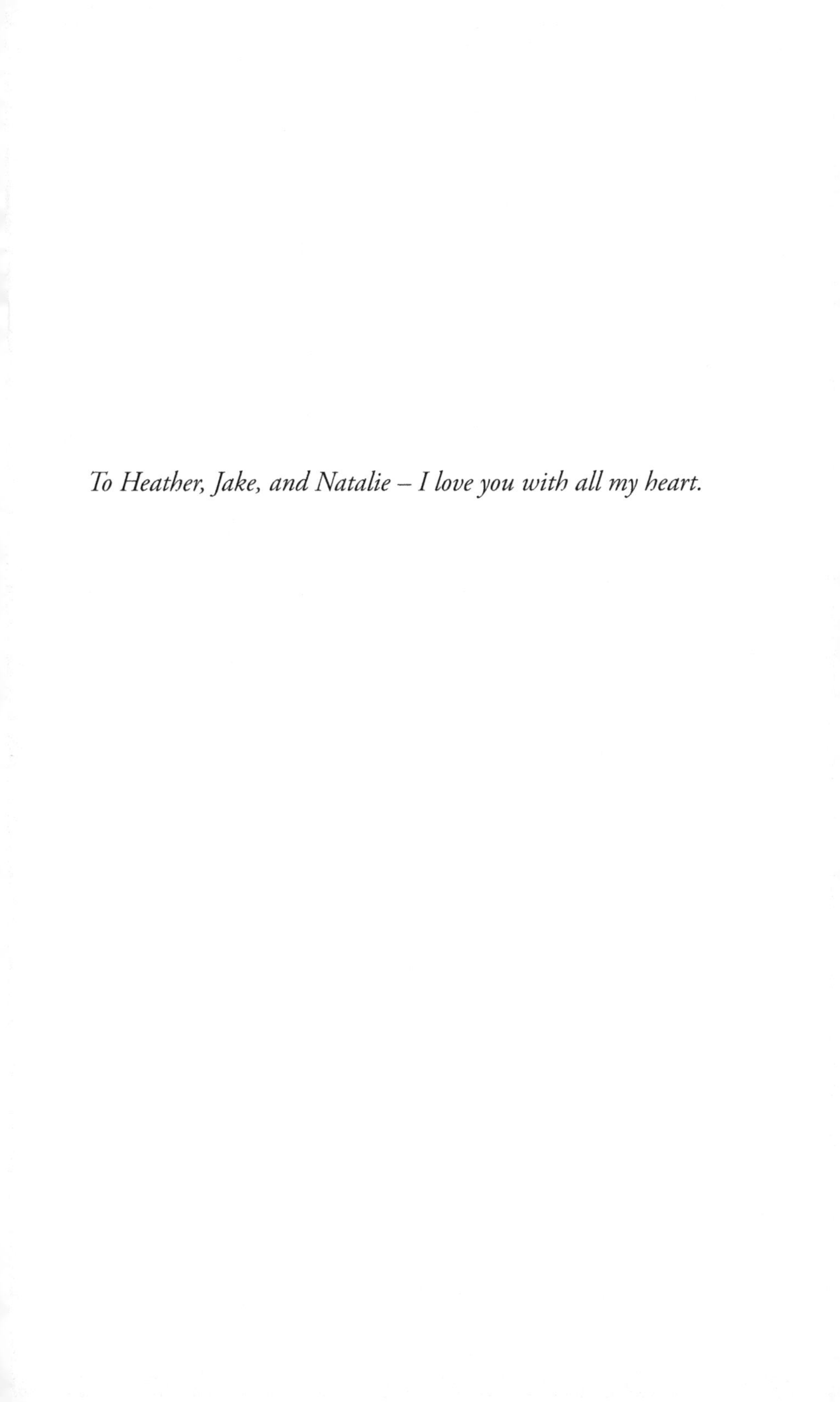

To Heather, Jake, and Natalie – I love you with all my heart.

Table of Contents

PART ONE

CHAPTER 1

Why Typical Financial Planning Has Failed

I know it was a dozen years ago, but I'll never forget what happened to my clients during the Great Recession of 2008. Part of the reason I'll never forget, aside from the pain it caused so many people, is that recessions, on average, occur at least once a decade. At this writing;, we've seen twelve consecutive years of growth. So what does that tell you about what could happen at almost any time?

When recessions hit, there's a lot of pain to go around. People lose their jobs. Retirement funds get slashed. And if you've retired and are living on a fixed income, it could take many years before you get back to where you were.

That's scary stuff, and yet pretty much every individual in our society is subject to the whims of the economy. If things start to go bad again, most people are defenseless.

Not *my* clients—but I don't want to get ahead of myself.

I'll tell you where I was in October 2008. I was already a successful financial advisor, and I thought I had the world by the tail. I had an economics degree and an MBA. I was a certified financial planner, and business was booming. I was happily married with two young children when a friend of mine approached and suggested we go on the trip of a lifetime: salmon fishing in the mountains of Alaska.

I was afraid to broach the subject with my wife because she was also working, not to mention helping take care of the kids and running the home. But I worked up my courage, and sure enough, she said, "Go on that trip. Everything will be fine here."

So there we were, my best buddy and I, salmon fishing in the mountains of Alaska. Bald eagles were flying everywhere, and we could see glaciers in the distance. The salmon were jumping and biting. It was paradise.

And then the market crashed.

Every hour, I would drive my truck from the river's edge to the top of a hill so I could get cell phone coverage and see how much the market had dropped since my last call. It was sickening. And here I was, isolated in the middle of nowhere. There was nothing I could do, although if I'd been back in the office, there was nothing I could have done there either.

That's when I realized that everything I knew about money was wrong.

I was sitting in a truck, surrounded by Alaskan glaciers, and all I could think about was my clients, especially the retirees. I was in my thirties, and I had no control of my money.

I had time to make up for the huge losses I'd just encountered, but what about my clients who didn't have another twenty or thirty years to grow their wealth back? What was going through their minds? Can you imagine having retired in 2006 or 2007 and helplessly watching your wealth—and your financial future—erode before your very eyes?

It just made no sense to me that the markets could come crashing down and destroy, in a day or a week or a month, everything that people had worked a lifetime to build. It didn't seem fair, and it didn't seem right.

And then I came to a second realization. While the middle class took a massive beating during the recession, the ultra-wealthy sailed through it. They didn't miss a beat. Their futures weren't threatened by the ups and downs of the market. Instead, they continued to enjoy enormous financial freedom and security.

It wasn't just that they had more money than other people.

It was what they did with their money.

They were in control.

When everyone else was losing their shirts, the most affluent members of society were actually compounding and growing their wealth.

How could this be?

More specifically, what could my clients do to enjoy the same sort of protection and growth—the same ability to ***control and compound*** their money—that the überwealthy took for granted?

This was the beginning of a journey in financial education that had nothing to do with anything I'd learned while getting my degree in economics, my MBA, or my financial planning certificate. I knew I couldn't put my clients' life savings and futures at risk ever again. There had to be a better way, and I had to find it. The strategies of Wall Street, the banks, and investment companies were not providing my clients with answers, so I had to find answers for myself.

The first realization I had, as I interviewed dozens upon dozens of people across North America who knew far more about investing than I did, was that everything I'd learned about investments had come from financial institutions, investment companies, and insurance companies. In other words, everything they taught financial advisors, like me, was biased, not necessarily accurate, and designed to benefit them—not our clients.

I decided to invest in myself. I spent six figures and a ton of time traveling, speaking with wealth advisors, and ultimately learning what wealthy people and business owners were doing with their money. I traveled throughout North America every month to learn from some of the top financial minds in the business.

I was amazed by how much they would share with me and what they could teach me, and here was my main takeaway: rich people were doing the exact opposite of what middle-class people did.

As one mentor put it, "If you want what the middle class has, which is fear of money, fear of running out of money, and fear of the stock market, do what they are doing. If you want to be like the wealthy, do what the wealthy do—the complete opposite of what the middle class does."

I felt like George Costanza in that Seinfeld episode where he decides that everything he has been doing is wrong, and he needs to do the exact opposite. It turned out to be true; the actions the wealthy took with their assets were the exact opposite of what the middle-class people did.

The middle class bought mutual funds, but they didn't make money with them. The only people who became millionaires with mutual funds were the financial advisors—and it was from the fees they charged, not from the returns those funds delivered.

So why were middle-class people investing in mutual funds? Because financial advisors, like me, had been practically brainwashed into teaching people that this was the only way to go.

To put it simply, middle-class people put their money at risk, while the wealthy put their money to work.

Over the course of that learning period, I discovered the strategies wealthy individuals had been using for over a century to grow, protect, and multiply their wealth. In this book, you will learn those secrets.

So, who is this book for?

This book is for the business owner, real estate investor, family, or individual who wants to take control of their money, multiply it, and compound it for the rest of their life.

This book is for those who want financial freedom.

CHAPTER 2

Hope Is Not a Strategy

Below is Retirement Mountain. It's composed of two very distinct phases: "Saving and Wealth Building" and "Income and Legacy." The top of Retirement Mountain is a peak. You climb a mountain to reach the top. You don't always think about going down again.

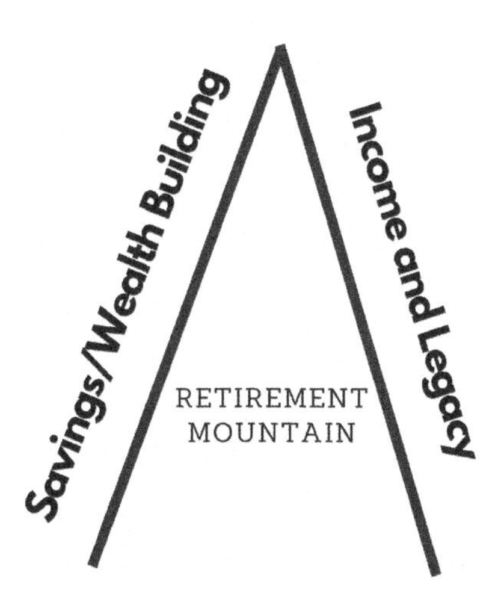

If you're like most people, you climb Retirement Mountain by putting your money in jail silos: RRSPs, RESPs, and TFSAs. You have no control. You can't take advantage of opportunities or emergencies.

Banks and Wall Street are in control. You roll the dice. You hope it all works out when you reach the top. You put all your energy into getting to the top, and you hope you have what it takes to get back to the bottom.

Just like when you climb a mountain, you're subject to the elements of nature. When you're accumulating money and putting it in these "money jails," you simply have no control of your money. Your strategy is hope: You hope that when you reach the top of Retirement Mountain, you'll have enough money to enjoy your golden years, your time in retirement.

The problem is that while you're on the way up the mountain, no one has told you what to do once you reach the peak! And the fact is, there are only two things you can do with your money: you can spend it, or you can give it away. That's it. There are no other choices. You can give it away while you're alive, or you can arrange how it will be distributed after you pass away. But when it comes to your money, those are the only options. Spend it, or give it away.

Let's first look at the spending side of the equation. You're at the top of Retirement Mountain, the peak of your life—the magical day when you don't have to work anymore.

Let's say you've saved a million dollars. Wow, a cool million! Good going, right? The problem is that if you were to look up at the sky, you might see dark clouds scudding across.

Those clouds are retirement risks. Let's name them: Taxes. Inflation. The possibility of long-term care. Market volatility. Fluctuation of interest rates. And the most significant risk of all: longevity. How can you possibly come down the mountain—de-accumulate or spend what you have—when you have no idea how long you and your spouse will live?

Longevity is the biggest risk of all, because it's a risk multiplier. The longer you live, the more likely you'll encounter repeated market downturns. The longer you live, the more likely taxes will go up. The longer you live, the more likely you or a spouse or partner will need long-term care. And the longer you live, the more likely inflation will eviscerate your holdings.

You want to get down the mountain safely, especially after you've put so much hard work into your ascent.

Retirement Risks:

1. **Market Volatility**
2. **Interest Rates**
3. **Taxes**
4. **Health Care/Long-Term Care**
5. **Inflation**
6. **Longevity**

Most people don't even think about these risks until they're ready to take an income. People are stuck with two ways to do so. One is to live off the interest and leave the capital alone. That's great if you've socked away a huge amount of money, but at today's low-interest-rate environment, 2 or 3 percent of $1 million does not produce much of an income.

The other broad category of "advice" you get from typical financial advisors is called Monte Carlo, or "safe distribution rate." If you know Monte Carlo, either from having visited there or just from the movies, you know that one of that beautiful French Riviera nation's most prominent features is a casino.

I'll never understand why the financial services industry has named its primary financial modeling system after a casino, where the patrons almost always lose and the house always wins—but in a weird way, it makes sense.

The Monte Carlo process is a modeling simulation that predicts how much money you can take out of what you own and have your money last for at least thirty years. The Monte Carlo method literally runs thousands upon thousands of simulations based upon interest rates and stock market performance to come up with a safe distribution or withdrawal rate.

Let me share an example of a Monte Carlo simulation. It's based on what we advisors used to call the 4 percent rule, before it got reduced. It's the idea that you could take 4 percent of your money out of your account and have it last throughout your retirement. For the sake of argument, let's imagine that you're sixty-five, and your risk tolerance indicates that you

Monte Carlo Simulation: 50% Stocks 50% Bonds @ 65

Withdrawal Rate	Probability of Running Out of Money
4%	57%
3%	24%

should invest 50 percent of your money in stocks, and the other 50 percent in bonds.

If we take out 4 percent of your money each year, you will have a 57 percent chance of failure—which is to say there's a 57 percent likelihood that you will run out of money within thirty years.

I don't know about you, but if I got on an airplane and the pilot announced, "There's a 57 percent chance of failure, but we hope to reach our destination anyway," I wouldn't take that flight! Would you? Hope is not a strategy for aviation any more than it is for financial services!

Let's say you took just 3 percent out of your account to live on every year. Now there's a 24 percent chance of failure. That's a one-in-four chance you'll run out of money while you're in retirement.

Is that how you want to live the rest of your life—in fear that you'll run out of money, and with the real possibility that it's exactly what will happen?

Let's go back to the idea that your investments will provide an income of $30,000 to $40,000 before tax. Now let's imagine you're a robust forty-five-year-old, twenty years away from retirement, and you're climbing Retirement Mountain. Assuming 3 percent inflation, you'll need to earn $180,000 a year in retirement to enjoy the same $100,000 lifestyle you have today.

Do you know how much you'll need to have in the bank by the time you're sixty-five to produce an income of $180,000? A cool $5 million.

How will you feel if you've been socking away $10,000 or $15,000 a year in retirement funds, and you're on your way to a million dollars in your RRSP, and your financial advisor tells you, "Good going on the saving. But at this rate, you're going to be $4 million short of what you'll need to keep your current lifestyle. Sorry to break the news."

Nobody wants to spend less in retirement. Sure, you may not be paying off the house any longer, and you probably will have taken care of your kids' education costs. But retirement is when people want to go see the world, visit the grandchildren, play golf, take cruises, or do whatever their hearts desire. You don't want to be scrimping and saving at that phase of your life, especially when you've worked so hard to put away all that money.

So who benefits when middle-class people lock up all their money in investments that don't get them to the finish line and don't get them down the mountain safely? That's right—the financial institutions, the insurance companies, the stockbrokers, and everyone else who collects fees on the money you've worked so hard to earn and save.

So far, we've been talking only about spending money. But what if you want to give it away? In that case, the typical middle-class approach to retirement—accumulating (savings) money going up Retirement Mountain and de-accumulating (spending) it as you go down the other side of the mountain—is even worse.

A new client once told me that he intended to leave each of his four children $250,000 from his RRSP. I had to be the bearer of bad news: of the million dollars he had saved in that RRSP, $540,000 would go to the CRA, leaving just $115,000 for each child.

He almost cried when I showed him the math. Did he want the government to be the largest beneficiary of his estate? What do you think?

In short, hope is a lousy strategy if you want to spend your money in retirement, and it's an even worse strategy if you want to give your money away. And as we've seen, spending it and giving it away are the only two things you can do with money, because as far as we know, you can't take it with you!

The problem is that with the typical middle-class model—and yes, having a million dollars in retirement means you are still firmly part of the middle class—you have only one economic power from which you can benefit: rate of return.

All the pressure on the typical Monte Carlo model that your advisor may have already shown you relates to the rate of return. If you don't get the rate of return you expect, your plan will collapse. And as we've seen, even if you do get the rate of return you desire, your failure rate is still awfully high.

Now let's look at a different approach to Retirement Mountain. We'll call this strategy "Certainty." This is the way the wealthy approach Retirement Mountain. And what separates the Hope strategy from the Certainty strategy that the wealthy use? These key words: ***control*** and ***compound***.

Unlike the middle class, wealthy people do not give up control of their money. They always maintain control. I'll show you how they do that. I'm just trying to get the basics into the discussion right now.

The second thing the wealthy enjoy, which most middle-class people never accomplish, is uninterrupted compounding. No matter how much wealthy people spend, their money magically grows anyway. They spent their entire life compounding.

Sound like a pipe dream? That's what your financial advisor and all the financial institutions in Canada want you to think, but it's not necessarily so. To put it simply, the wealthy ***control and compound*** their money, while the middle class lives in a world of fear and fees.

I'll tell you one more thing wealthy people do with their money. They make it do more than one job at the same time. Middle-class folks have to make choices—save or invest, invest in retirement or pay off the mortgage, and so on. Wealthy people function almost like banks, in that banks can do multiple things with money. Again, I'll show you how. I'm just trying to get everything on the table! Wealthy people act like banks when it comes to their money, while middle-class people act like bank customers—always getting walloped on fees and never getting rich.

Who would you rather be, the middle-class individual trying to make it safely down the dangerous Retirement Mountain with little income, or the wealthy individual who practically glides down with certainty? I thought so.

In this book, I'm going to show you the strategies that the wealthy use to ***control and compound*** their money. This will put at your disposal the same four economic powers the wealthy already enjoy—rate of return, actuarial science, tax diversification, and uncorrelated assets—and I'll explain each one as we move along.

Best of all, you'll be in control of your money, allowing you to accumulate more wealth on your way up the mountain. And because you'll have all four of these economic powers at your side, you'll be able to spend 7 to 12 percent of your money—instead of just 3 to 4 percent—while at the same time eliminating or reducing most retirement risks.

Sound appealing? I thought so. Now let me show you how it works.

CHAPTER 3

Understanding Two Big Traps: The Stock Market and RRSPs

Okay, friends, take out a pen and paper, because it's time to do a little math, the kind that Wall Street, Bay Street, and financial institutions have been using for years—to pull the wool over our eyes. It reminds me of a wonderful quote attributed to Benjamin Disraeli about how in our world, "There are three kinds of lies: lies, damned lies, and statistics."

What I'm about to show you fits into any of these three categories!

Let me ask you a simple question. I'm going to give you two numbers: six and eight. What's the average?

Of course, it's seven. Right now you're asking me, "How dumb do you think I am?"

I don't think you're dumb. I think you're pretty smart. The problem is, the financial institutions think you aren't that bright. Let me show you why.

If I told you we were talking about a 6 percent rate of return in one year and an 8 percent rate of return in another year, you would tell me that we have an average rate of return of 7 percent. But let me give you a slightly more complicated problem:

In year one, let's say your investment goes up 100 percent. Nice, right?

Then in year two, unfortunately, it drops by 50 percent. Uh-oh.

In year three, we're back on track. It goes up 100 percent again. Feeling good, huh? Of course you are!

And now in year four, things look a lot like year two. Our return is minus 50 percent.

So how would you calculate the average rate of return for those four years? Up a hundred, down fifty, up a hundred, down fifty. Most people would conclude that we achieved an average rate of return over those four years of 25 percent. We add up the numbers to get 100 and divide by 4.

Now, if your advisor came to you and said that she was averaging a 25 percent return on your portfolio, you'd most likely be turning cartwheels! Your advisor would be asking for a list of referrals, and you'd be singing her praises to everyone you've ever met because she was just killing it with your investments.

But not so fast! Let's look at what really happened over the course of those four years.

Let's say we started with $100,000 and doubled it—a 100 percent return—in year one. At the end of the year, we have $200,000.

But in year two, we lose half our money, which takes us back down to . . . that's right . . . $100,000 again.

Doubling it again in year three brings us back to $200,000. Happy days!

Unfortunately, the market tanks again in year four, taking us down 50 percent, back to . . . that's right . . . our original $100,000.

Our average rate of return was indeed 25 percent. But our actual rate of return was . . . wait for it . . . 0 percent. (If you're old enough to remember *Animal House,* you may recall that was Bluto's midterm grade.)

Which do you care about more? The average rate of return, which is a stratospherically high 25 percent, or that miserable actual rate of return: 0?

If you're like most people, the number that really sings to you is the average rate of return. But here in the real world, your portfolio is measured by the actual rate.

Average vs. Actual Rate of Return

Year	% Return	End of Year Balance
1	+100%	$200,000
2	-50%	$100,000
3	+100%	$200,000
4	-50%	$100,000

Average Return: 25%	Actual Return: 0%

Now I'm not saying the stock market really goes up 100 percent and down 50 percent every two years. But if you look at the next chart, the S&P 500 index actually went up a little more than a 100 percent . . . and then down 50 percent . . . and then up 100 percent again . . . and then down a little more than 50 percent. Over the first twelve-year period depicted in this chart, an investor who had gone along for that dizzying ride would actually be in the red.

Now, from 2009 to the present, ever since my Alaska fishing trip, the market has been on an eleven-year bull run, up over 378 percent. It's only been one of the greatest bull runs of all time!

And what do you think is going to happen next? To put it in another way, is this the time to be putting money into the stock market?

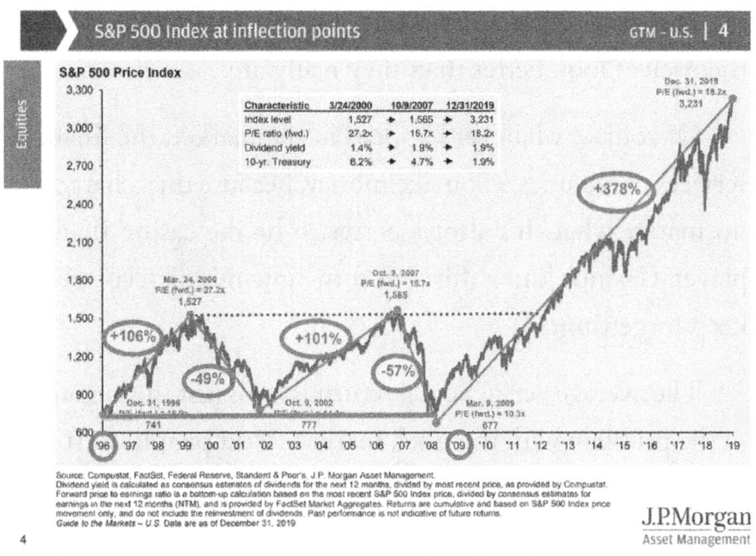

Credit: J.P. Morgan Asset Management and Guide to the Markets [Q4 2019]

If you don't mind the downtimes that follow the uptimes, invest all the money you want in the stock market. I wouldn't do it, but I can't stop you.

That's the first problem we have with stocks: financial firms typically speak only about average rates of return, while here in the real world, people have to deal with actual returns.

Will you ever hear an investment firm touting actual rate of return? Not in this lifetime. Whereas zero doesn't have a very nice ring to it, you can massage the numbers to create an average rate of return that sounds like you're setting the world on fire.

And that's what some financial firms are claiming, making themselves look better than they really are.

Of course, whatever happens in the market, the financial services companies will make money, because they charge fees no matter what. It's always better to be the casino than the player. Casinos know this, but somehow middle-class people keep forgetting.

The average versus actual return issue is just the beginning of the problem with the stock market. Most people don't pick individual stocks. They invest in mutual funds or segregated funds. The chart below shows how many of those funds actually beat the index.

All those ads you see for funds are those that beat the index in any given year. But the financial services firms offer dozens or even hundreds of funds. Statistically, something will beat the market for some period of time. But over the long haul, it's not the same.

In the Canadian dividend and equity category, over a ten-year period, 0 percent of mutual funds beat the index. Zero! If you look at the U.S. equity category over that same time period, 97 percent of the funds failed to beat the index.

The good news for these funds is that they make money off fees regardless of whether or not they beat the index. Well, its good news for them, not you. The wealthy do not put money in mutual funds, and now you know why.

REPORTS

Report 1: Percent of Active Funds Underperforming Index

This report shows the percentage of funds that have underperformed their comparable benchmarks over 1-, 3-, 5-, and 10-year periods. The comparison starts with the funds in a category at the beginning of the period. At the end of the period, the report shows what percentage of funds have underperformed their benchmark. The fund's category at the end of the period is not considered because the category at the beginning of the holding period is of interest.

Most reports that purport to show the percent of active funds underperforming an index work with the funds in a category at the end of the period and then compare their historical returns to the benchmark. The SPIVA Canada Scorecard corrects for this survivorship bias by starting with the funds at the beginning of the period.

Report 1: Percentage of Funds Underperforming the Index

FUND CATEGORY	COMPARISON INDEX	1-YEAR (%)	3-YEAR (%)	5-YEAR (%)	10-YEAR (%)
Canadian Equity	S&P/TSX Composite	85.45	94.37	88.00	88.06
Canadian Small-/Mid-Cap Equity	S&P/TSX Completion	87.88	88.57	78.05	70.69
Canadian Dividend & Income Equity	S&P/TSX Canadian Dividend Aristocrats	88.00	65.38	73.68	100.00
U.S. Equity	S&P 500 (CAD)	74.00	85.59	93.33	98.17
International Equity	S&P EPAC LargeMidCap (CAD)	54.35	95.08	79.66	87.72
Global Equity	S&P Developed LargeMidCap (CAD)	80.00	87.27	90.80	95.83
Canadian Focused Equity	50% S&P/TSX Composite + 25% S&P 500 (CAD) + 25% S&P EPAC LargeMidCap	79.71	96.67	98.00	97.84

Source: S&P Dow Jones Indices LLC, Fundata. Data as of June 30, 2019. CIFSC categorizations are used. Financial information provided by Fundata Canada Inc. Past performance is no guarantee of future results. Table is provided for illustrative purposes.

Source: SPIVA® Canada Mid-Year 2019 Scorecard.
S&P Dow Jones Indices. Data as of June 30, 2019.

So how do members of the middle class save their money? It looks like this.

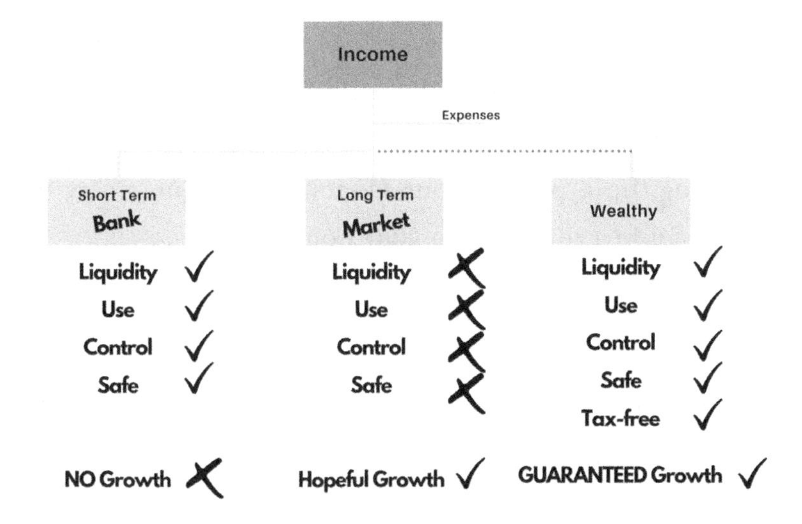

They separate their savings into two categories. They want to make sure their short-term savings is safe, liquid, and accessible anytime. Typically, this is a bank account earning no growth.

Remember what Robert Kiyosaki said in *Rich Dad Poor Dad*: "Savers are losers." When you save money in a bank account, your interest is 100 percent taxable. And the interest paid, if any, does not even keep up with inflation. So, every time you put dollars in a bank account, you lose and fall behind; the wealthy and the banks know this.

And then members of the middle class have a second place they save money that they really do not have any control over—no liquidity, unsafe, and with only "hopeful" growth—and that is typically the stock market. We will see in Part Two of this book that the wealthy consider money one large pool of wealth and save much differently.

What could be a smarter, safer, more resilient, more effective investment than a mutual fund? Actually, pretty much anything, from putting your money under your pillow to burying it in a coffee can in your front yard.

Now let's talk about RRSPs. Let's say a fast-talking guy in a shiny suit strolls into your office and tells you he wants to go into business with you.

"OK," you ask, "how is this going to work?"

He grabs a seat, puts his arm around a chair, leans back, and says, "We're going to go into business, but I'm going to set the rules. There are five rules you need to know:

"Number one, you need to put up all the money. Number two, you need to take all the risks. Number three, you will pay all the fees. Number four, you have no control or access to the money until you retire. And number five, let's leave the ownership somewhat vague. How does that sound?"

It sounds terrible, right? Yet this is what millions of well-meaning Canadians do whenever they sock money away in an RRSP.

Who's the partner? The government, of course.

Who puts up all the money? You.

Who takes all the risk that the investment vehicles you choose will not make money over time, or that the market will be down when you need your money? You.

Who pays all the fees? Certainly not the bank or the government. Must be you again.

Who controls the whole process? The government and the financial institutions. Not you.

And why is the ownership vague if it's your money? The government has every right to raise taxes on the withdrawals you'll make decades from now—because it's the government! It has the taxing power, and for the most part, over time, taxes go up, never down. So even the ownership of the money in your RRSP is vague and subject to change, because the government can keep as much as it wants down the road simply by pushing a new tax increase through Parliament.

You're probably saying that if that slick-talking guy came into your office offering a deal like that, you'd throw him out on the spot. But, actually, only the wealthy would do that.

Middle-class people, by contrast, line up for it. They feel they're doing the right thing with their money, that putting it in an RRSP is better than having it all go to consumption.

But when you really think about the rules of the road for RRSPs, maybe you should start to think more like the wealthy, who rarely fall into this trap.

Middle-class Canadians typically believe that RRSPs are tax deductible, but that's a misconception. RRSPs only defer tax; you pay the tax when you take your money out. Everybody says, "It's OK, I'll be in a lower tax bracket by the time I retire." So let me get something straight: You're counting on making less money and living on less money after you retire? That doesn't sound like a lot of fun.

Let me give you a clear example of how useless, to be frank, RRSPs can be. Take a look at the chart on the following page. John is in a 30 percent tax bracket. He deposits $20,000 into his RRSP. His money grows at 5 percent a year over the next twenty-five years, so the future value is $67,727.

Mary, on the other hand, pays the 30 percent tax on her $20,000 today, leaving her with $14,000 to invest. She sticks the money in a tax-free vehicle that earns the same 5 percent, and over twenty-five years it grows to $47,409.

Twenty-five years from today, who has more money, John or Mary?

Instinctively, you want to say John. But, in fact, he doesn't.

Remember that RRSPs are a tax-deferral device, not a tax-deduction device. When John takes that $67, 727 out of his RRSP, and he's still in a 30 percent tax bracket, he'll be down to $47,409, the same amount as Mary.

But what if John is in a higher tax bracket in twenty-five years? Remember, taxes typically go up, not down. Let's say the government now wants 40 percent instead of 30 percent. Now John's nest egg is only $40,636, more than $7,000 below Mary's.

John's RRSP Withdrawal—Year 25

Tax Rate	Net After Tax
30%	$47,409
40%	$40,636
50%	$33,863

The tax-deferral strategy failed because over time, taxes went up, which is what they typically do. Just as importantly, John gave up control of his money. For twenty-five years, he was unable to take advantage of opportunities that came along, or to handle emergencies that might have arisen because his money was locked up in RRSP jail.

That's right! When you put your money in an RRSP, you basically put it in jail. And as for the fabrication about being in a lower tax bracket when you retire, let me get this straight. You're looking for a financial advisor who will ensure you have less income and less wealth twenty-five years from now than you do today so you can pay less in taxes? If that's how you feel, this book may not be for you!

Your marginal tax rate may indeed go down if the amount of money you take out of your investments in retirement each year is lower than your preretirement income. But what's typically left out of this equation is what I call the Gotcha Tax. It's a tax most people don't know about until they turn sixty-five and retire; only by then, it's too late.

The actual name of the Gotcha Tax is the Old Age Security (OAS) clawback. If you're over sixty-five in Canada and you have an income of roughly $75,000, you are subject to the OAS clawback, which is essentially a tax placed on what you would receive in OAS.

If you want to see the actual numbers, visit my website, www.controlandcompound.com. For the sake of simplicity, the OAS clawback means that even though you are paying a lower rate of income tax, your actual tax is higher because of the clawback.

The OAS clawback alone is enough to put most affluent middle-class retirees into a higher effective tax bracket than they'd ever imagined.

Gotcha.

Actually, that's only one type of Gotcha Tax. There's also the senior age credit, both provincial and federal, which you'll lose above a certain amount of income. Many provinces have a seniors' drug plan in which your income determines your payment or your deductible. Long-term care in many provinces is based upon taxable income, so the cost is a function of what you earn.

Marginal Tax Rate (MTR) While Working and Retired

Working Income	MTR While Working	Retired Income	MTR @ 65+ Retired	MTR @ 65+ OAS Clawback
$60,000	37.17%	$40,000	29.95%	29.95%
$80,000	37.17%	$60,000	37.17%	37.17%
$100,000	43.50%	$80,000	37.17%	52.17%
$140,000	46.5%	$105,000	43.50%	58.50%
$200,000	50%	$100,000	43.50%	58.50%

The more you make, the bigger the Gotcha Taxes. And again, it's highly unlikely that you'll be in a lower tax bracket down the road, or that tax rates will be lower by the time you retire.

Why am I so certain that taxes will increase in the future? Because of Canada's aging population, government debt, and increasing health-care costs.

The Fraser Institute created an excellent report titled *Canada's Aging Population and Implications for Government Finances,* by Taylor Jackson, Jason Clemens, and Milagros Palacios, who examined the government's future expenditures and revenues.

Based on their projections, government revenues will be flat. But with more baby boomers retiring, working less, and earning less, expenditures are destined to rise.

Elderly benefits to cover old-age security and guaranteed income supplements? Up.

Health-care spending on a per-person basis? Way up.

Who's going to pay for it? Taxpayers. And even in retirement, if you are earning money from your investments, you, my friend, are still a taxpayer—and that's especially true if you have RRSP or RRIF income.

Yet financial institutions and the government are falling all over each other in trying to convince you, like that slick-talking guy in the earlier example, that nothing could be better for you than a tax-deferred investment vehicle, like an RRSP or RRIF.

Does it make sense to defer a lower tax rate today in order to pay higher taxes down the road? The middle class takes that deal every day of the week. But do you think the wealthy go in for a bad bargain like that? Of course not.

So now you've seen that the stock market and the financial institutions that are constantly trying to get you to invest in the stock market and RRSPs are not really operating in your best interest. And, unfortunately, the same thing is true when it comes to the government and the retirement accounts it pushes on the middle class.

If you think for a minute that wealthy people put their futures at risk in these ways, you have another thing coming. They don't. You cannot ***control and compound*** your money, which is what the wealthy do, when it's locked up in jail, where you can't touch it, as with RRSPs and RRIFs, or where it's subject to the rise and fall of the stock market. The wealthy are too smart for that.

But before we can really understand what they do to make their money grow, no matter what's happening in the world around them, we need to have a better understanding of the wealth destroyers the rest of us face. That's what we'll examine in the next chapter.

CHAPTER 4

Meet the Wealth Destroyers

In this world, there are four great wealth destroyers. If you don't tame them, your chances of becoming wealthy, or even *wealthier,* are slim.

Good old, long-lost great-aunt Mildred. You've never heard of her, but one day you get the wonderful news that a hundred years ago, she set up a trust fund for her heirs. And guess what? You're the only heir the government can identify!

A century ago, she put aside $7,257, and she was canny enough to find a guaranteed return of 10 percent. Now a hundred years have gone by, and the money in that account has grown to . . . wait for it . . . $100 million.

100 Years of Tax-Free 10% Growth

Year	Value
1	$7,982
20	$48,819
40	$328,427
60	$2,209,493
80	$14,864,363
100	$100,000,000

Happy days, right? Pretty cool, right? Couldn't you do a lot of good things with a hundred million bucks? Wouldn't this be amazing for your family if this happened? Couldn't you set your family up for generations to come, thanks to your wonderful, brilliant, long-lost great-aunt Mildred?

We're all familiar with the concept that if one takes a small amount of anything and doubles it every day for thirty days, there won't be much growth in the first ten days, but in the last twenty, the growth will be stratospheric.

That's the magic of compound interest. Mildred was patient. After all, she had a hundred-year span to play with! Due to the compounding of the 10 percent a year she was making, the growth wasn't spectacular in the first ten or twenty years after she invested the money. But after that, year after year for eighty years, the return was absolutely unbelievable. Her money was making 10 percent on the 10 percent on the

10 percent on the 10 percent and so on. That's how we got from $7,257 to $100 million.

Now here's the bad news: your great-aunt Mildred didn't live in a no-tax country, like the Cayman Islands. Instead, she lived in Canada, where her money was taxed at 50 percent. Year after year, the government took half her growth out of that investment. How much do you think that cost you? Would you guess fifteen million dollars? Twenty million dollars? Fifty million dollars? Well, let's take a look.

1. Taxes

Your number one wealth destroyer is taxes. If your great-aunt Mildred's investment has been taxed at a rate of 50 percent from the time she started it, you will not be getting a cheque for $100 million. Instead, you'll get a cheque for just $1 million.

A million dollars out of the blue is terrific, but it's not $100 million!

So let that sink in. You lost 99 percent of what you would have received if there'd been no tax. Many business owners and individuals pay too much tax unknowingly and unnecessarily year after year, but the real pain isn't from wasted tax dollars; it's from what those tax dollars could have grown to over time.

It might not be $99 million for you, but it probably adds up to hundreds of thousands or even a few million, depending on how much you earn. Tax is the single biggest destroyer of wealth.

I'll say it again because I really want you to grasp that fact: tax is the number one destroyer of wealth.

2. Fees

The number two wealth destroyer is fees. Let's go back to your great-aunt Mildred and our $100 million fund.

Let's say Milly had paid 0 percent in fees. Of the $100 million, how much is left? That's right—$100 million!

But what if she'd paid a 2 percent fee over all this time to the investment company? Instead of $100 million, you'd have only $13 million. In other words, fees would have cost you more than $87 million out of the $100 million.

When you hear 1 percent or 2 percent, you say to yourself, "That's not that much. What's the big deal?"

Well, $87 million is an awfully big deal. And again, maybe we're not talking about that many zeroes in your financial situation. But the reality is that you are losing *mucho dinero* every year to fees. And since the money that's lost to fees isn't being compounded, you're losing even more. And that's money you never even realized you could have had.

3. Volatility

The number three wealth destroyer is volatility. Check out the chart below. As we saw in the stock market example in the previous chapter, when we compared average returns to actual returns, negative returns significantly impact overall results.

Let's say your great-aunt Mildred's investment had been hit with a negative 40 percent return every fifteen years, meaning that Mildred's investment had dropped 40 percent at years fifteen, thirty, forty-five, sixty, seventy-five, and ninety. In this example, assuming no fees and no tax, the volatility alone would cost us over $97 million.

The Effect of 100 Years of Wealth Destroyers

Year	No Tax, Fee, or Volatility	Just 50% Tax	Just 2% Fee	Just Volatility
100	$100,000,000	$954,248	$13,261,956	$2,633,610

What if you had taxes, fees, and volatility? $66,300, with 99.93 percent lost to wealth destroyers. (For full chart with all years, please go to www.controlan-dcompound.com.)

You might be saying, "Darren, you're talking about a hundred years. I don't have a hundred-year window for my investments. Why is this relevant to me?" OK, fine. Let's take another example of a much shorter period, using actual numbers from the S&P 500.

From 2000 to 2019 the average return of the S&P 500 was 7.31 percent. Based on that average return, if you invested roughly $250,000 in 2000, you'd have a million dollars twenty years later. That's Financial Planning 101, right? A typical financial advisor takes the money you have, plugs in a rate of return, and forecasts what you will have down the road.

In this case, your money grew by approximately $750,000 using the actual rate of return. But as we've seen, actual rate of return does not include our wealth destroyers. If we use the same numbers over this same twenty-year period and include a tax rate of 25 percent and fees of 2 percent, while plugging in the actual rates of return—not the average, but the actual—we experience a much different outcome.

S&P 500 Market History

Average Rate of Return	7.31%
Year	**S&P 500 with Dividends**
2000	(9.07)
2001	(11.85)
2002	(21.98)
2003	28.45
2004	10.87
2005	4.92
2006	15.68
2007	5.51
2008	(36.63)
2009	25.85
2010	14.89
2011	2.23
2012	16.00
2013	32.23

2014	13.63
2015	1.46
2016	11.85
2017	21.64
2018	(4.28)
2019	24.91

$243,891 at Average 7.31% Return

Year	Account Value	Rate	Account Value
1	$243,891	7.31%	$261,720
2	$261,720	7.31%	$280,851
3	$280,851	7.31%	$301,382
4	$301,382	7.31%	$323,413
5	$323,413	7.31%	$347,054
6	$347,054	7.31%	$372,424
7	$372,424	7.31%	$399,648
8	$399,648	7.31%	$428,862
9	$428,862	7.31%	$460,212
10	$460,212	7.31%	$493,853
11	$493,853	7.31%	$529,954
12	$529,954	7.31%	$568,694
13	$568,694	7.31%	$610,265
14	$610,265	7.31%	$654,876
15	$654,876	7.31%	$702,747
16	$702,747	7.31%	$754,118
17	$754,118	7.31%	$809,244
18	$809,244	7.31%	$868,400
19	$868,400	7.31%	$931,880
20	$931,880	7.31%	$1,000,000

Actual Return with Taxes, Fees, and Volatility
1.5% Actual Return

Year	Account Value	Earnings Rate	End of Year Account Value
1	$243,891	(9.07%)	$217,335
2	$217,335	(11.85%)	$187,743
3	$187,743	(21.98%)	$143,546
4	$143,546	28.45%	$171,407
5	$171,407	10.87%	$182,528
6	$182,528	4.92%	$186,387
7	$186,387	15.68%	$205,066
8	$205,066	5.51%	$210,295
9	$210,295	(36.63%)	$130,596
10	$130,596	25.85%	$153,449
11	$153,449	14.89%	$167,943
12	$167,943	2.23%	$168,172
13	$168,172	16.00%	$185,432
14	$185,432	32.23%	$226,584
15	$226,584	13.63%	$245,882
16	$245,882	1.46%	$244,476
17	$244,476	11.85%	$262,096
18	$262,096	21.64%	$299,854
19	$299,854	(4.28%)	$281,272
20	$281,272	24.91%	$328,551

Take a look at the chart above. Our money grew to only $328,000, a gain of approximately $75,000 instead of $750,000.

In short, taxes, fees, and volatility cost you 90 percent of your growth. Do you think the wealthy subject their investments to taxes, fees, and volatility? Of course they don't.

4. Interrupting Compound Interest

So far in this chapter, we've discussed three wealth destroyers—taxes, fees, and volatility. Interrupting the compound interest is the fourth wealth destroyer, and in many ways, it's the worst of all.

Take a look at the next chart, which is an exponential growth curve. On the x-axis—that is to say, the left-hand side—we have dollars. On the y-axis—on the bottom—we have time.

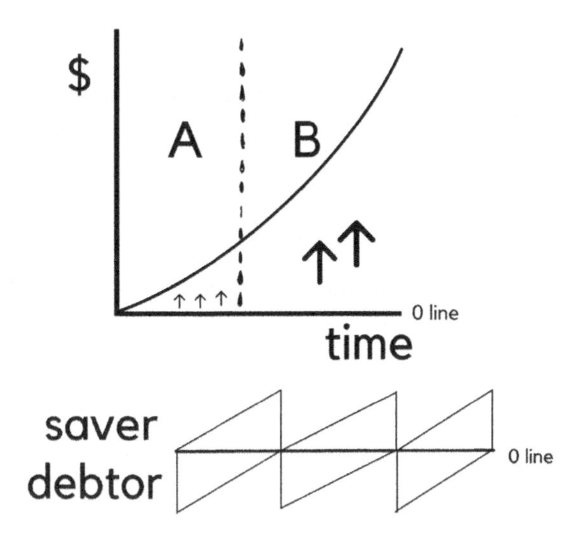

If you had to pick either side A, where returns are small, or side B, where returns are large, which side would you want to be on? Side B, of course.

But most people get stuck on side A, near zero. We call them debtors . . . or savers. And in many ways, these practices amount to the same thing.

Debtors borrow money and then pay it off over time, as with a car loan. Or they borrow money for a down payment on a real estate transaction and then pay off the loan. But they end up at the zero line, because once the loan is paid off, they get a bigger car or a bigger property, they start borrowing again, and they have no benefit of compound interest. Not good, right?

If you're prudent, you're probably saying that people should save up their money before they buy anything. Pay cash, and then you avoid interest charges, right?

You may think you're smarter than the debtors, but not so fast! Savers hang on to their money and then pay cash for the car or the down payment or whatever. In other words, once they've got enough to buy whatever they want to buy, they go back to the zero line. They may not be paying interest, but they aren't compounding their money.

One of my mentors, R. Nelson Nash, taught me that you finance everything you buy, and you never take a big chunk of your money out of the bank to pay for something—because that's when your money stops compounding. As we saw with Great-Aunt Mildred's investment, failure to compound cripples the growth of wealth.

Now, we all understand that debtors pay interest on what they buy. That's common knowledge. But most people don't realize that savers end up in the same place as debtors—which is to say, the zero line—because they may not be paying interest, but they're giving up growth.

They're giving up the possibility of what their dollars could have become. And they don't even realize what they've lost, because they never stopped to think what their money could've done for them if only they'd financed the purchase and kept on compounding their investment! They're too busy congratulating themselves on being prudent to recognize that they've ended up in the same lousy place as the debtor.

Let me give you an example.

Let's say you need $40,000 for an opportunity, a new car, or an emergency, and you've been saving for this day. You cash out your savings and use your money to pay in cash. What just happened to your long-term wealth? You interrupted its compounding by paying cash for a major purchase/investment. Now you have guaranteed you will not have uninterrupted compounding. You are restarting the compounding, and you never made it out of side A. It's helpful to look at this chart at each of the five referenced points

1. You have saved $40,000, and you are just starting to see nice gains as you inch up the compound curve.

2. You cash out your investment and go back to zero, interrupting compounding—and then restart the compounding from the zero line.

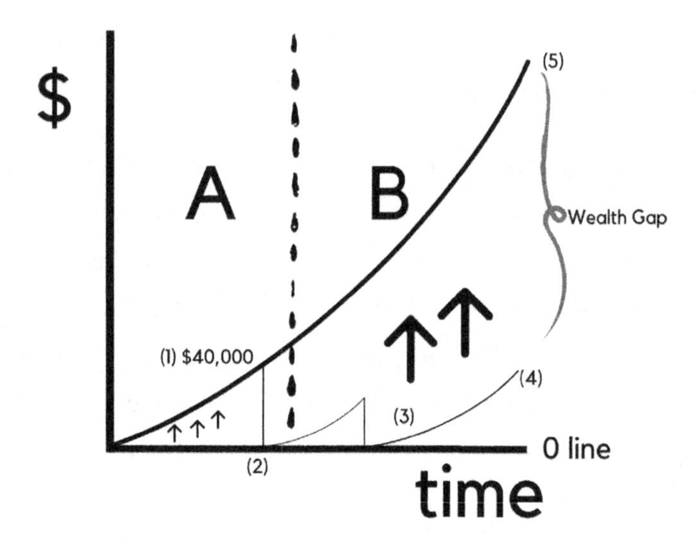

3. The stock market where you invested has a little dip.

4. This is where you end up at the end.

5. This is where the wealthy end up—those who did not interrupt the compound curve.

I cannot stress how important it is to tame these four wealth destroyers (taxes, fees, volatility, and interrupting compound interest). I want to show you one more example to make sure stopping these wealth destroyers becomes a major focus of your wealth building.

Some people will be familiar with this penny example, but I have added the wealth destroyers to illustrate how they attack your wealth and why you need to be diligent in your efforts to eliminate them.

We are going to start with a penny and double it every day for a month to show the impact of these four wealth destroyers.

1. Marie doubles her penny every day but pays a 2 percent *fee*—$5,857,093 at end of month.

2. Jim *interrupts* his compounding in day 21 by paying cash for a car and resetting the compounding to the 0 line—$2.56 at end of month.

3. Natalie doubles her pennies every day but has three days of *volatility*—a 40 percent return on days 10, 20, and 30—$289,910 at end of month.

4. Jake pays 50 percent *tax* on the growth of his penny—$1,918 at end of month.

If you were able to find a way to pay no tax, pay no fees, have no volatility, and not have to interrupt the compound curve every time you need access to money, you would have $10,737,418 at the end of the month. Just look at what each one of these wealth destroyers costs you. I say *you,* because the wealthy have figured out how to avoid, drastically reduce, or eliminate these wealth destroyers.

So how do you avoid that fate?

You've seen all the ways middle-class people lose money or fail to make what they can if they're not led down the garden path by the government, financial institutions, and banks. Now let me show you exactly how banks make money—because wealthy people make money the same way banks do.

Once you understand how banks earn their money, you'll be on the path to being the bank instead of being the bank customer. And, as, bank robber Willie Sutton said, that's where the money is!

CHAPTER 5

How Banks and the Wealthy Make Money (and How You Can Too!)

Master motivator Tony Robbins says, "If you want to be successful, find someone who has achieved the results you want and copy what they do, and you'll achieve the same results." In other words, success leaves clues.

Who makes money in our society? Financial institutions—specifically, banks. Wealthy people and corporations long ago came to the realization that if they want to make money, they should act like banks. So in this chapter, we'll examine the three ways banks make money.

First, they arrange to receive money systematically.

Second, they want to hold on to new money as long as they possibly can.

Third, when they give it back, they want to pay it out as slowly as possible.

Getting money systematically means that banks have methodologies for receiving money. You get paid twice a month, which means the bank receives money twice a month. You pay your mortgage or car loan monthly, which means the bank gets money monthly. And so on. Same thing with credit cards.

And, of course, if you're late with a mortgage payment, car payment, or credit card payment, you know what happens: fees—and those fees only get higher and higher. Yes, banks are very smart about getting money on a systematic basis.

Banks want to hold on to money for as long as possible. Consider RRSPs. If you're industrious, you open an RRSP in your twenties, and the money stays with the bank for forty years! That's a pretty good deal, when you come to think of it. Who else can get to keep money for almost half a century before having to pay out a dime?

Finally, banks want to drip money back to you instead of cutting you a big cheque. Ever try to take a large amount of money out of a bank? You'll be standing there for an awfully long time while they verify that it's really you, even if you have been going to that branch for twenty years. Maybe they're hoping that if they keep you standing there for half an hour, you'll change your mind!

Seriously, most people take out only small amounts each year from their RRSPs/RRIFs in retirement. That's how banks like it. Receive it on a systematic basis, keep it for as long as possible, and dole it out in dribs and drabs.

In addition to these three strategies for getting and holding on to money, banks have three rules they follow religiously: cash flow, leverage, and the velocity of money. Let's look at each in turn.

Take a look at the following graphic, in which Samantha goes to the bank and deposits a hundred dollars. She will probably receive less than half of 1 percent of interest per year on her money, but for the sake of round figures, let's call it 1 percent. The bank then lends the money to someone else at a much higher rate. It could be a mortgage at 4 percent, a business loan at 8 percent, a second mortgage at 12 percent, or even a credit card at 22 percent.

For the sake of argument, let's use a figure of 10 percent and say the bank loaned this money to John. That might be a little high, but it makes the math more straightforward so we can more easily understand the concept.

How much did the bank make in a year on Samantha's $100? Most people would say that it paid out 1 percent and charged 10 percent to John, so its return was 9 percent. That's a pretty good return, wouldn't you say? How many places can you think of where you can get a 9 percent return on your money right now?

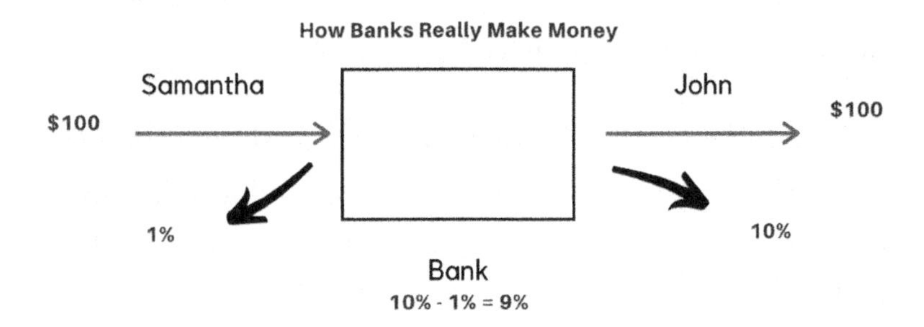

Well, truth be told, the bank made a heck of a lot more than that.

Now let's look at the next graphic. The bank never actually loaned out its money. Instead, it loaned Samantha's money. In other words, it bought the use of Samantha's hundred dollars for the cost of one dollar, and it sold it for 10 percent, which is ten dollars. If you buy something for one dollar and you sell it for ten dollars, your actual rate of return is 900 percent. Nine hundred percent! What a return!

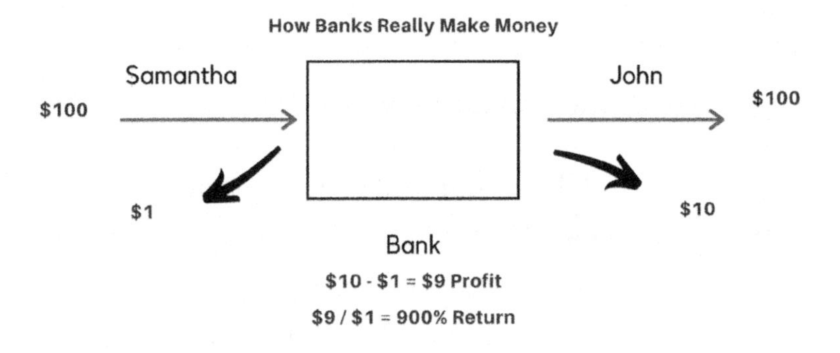

Wouldn't it be cool to act like a bank and make a 900 percent return? Do you see why wealthy people choose to act like banks? Getting 900 percent on your money is a good day at the office; wouldn't you agree?

But the bank is just getting started!

It can actually have that one dollar do more than one job. It can take the hundred dollars Samantha deposited and loan it to the person with the mortgage on his house, loan it to a business owner, loan it to the person taking a second mortgage, and then loan it to the person with the credit card. In other words, the money is doing more than one job, which multiplies that 900 percent return many times over.

This is exactly what wealthy people do with their money. Banks don't like to have money just sitting there. They like to loan it out, and they like to have it do more than one job. The proper term for this phenomenon is "financial velocity."

Middle-class people treat money as what I call an *or* asset, because they can do this *or* that with it. They can spend it, *or* they can save it. But they can't do more than one thing with it. Banks and wealthy people treat money as an *and* asset, because they can do this *and* that with the money. They can loan it out to A as a mortgage, *and* they can loan it out to B as credit card debt. Pretty nifty, huh?

As I've said from the outset, wealthy people act like banks, while the middle class acts like bank customers.

Banks are getting a phenomenal return on their money because it is an *and* asset, not an *or* asset. They're getting cash flow. They're getting leverage by using the money repeatedly. And they've got a high velocity of money because they're able to use the money repeatedly.

Just like a bank, you can multiply your money without market risk, investment risk, or tax risk. Your money will be growing inside the investment, and you can have money working for you outside the investment.

With the banking system, all the money is constantly flowing away from you. Your income gets deposited into a bank, and it flows to bills, mortgages, retirement savings, credit cards, loans, cell phone bills, and more. When you are the bank, all that money flows back to you, and you recapture all that interest.

The bank wants money in motion. If your blood does not circulate, you die. If oxygen does not circulate, you die. If water does not circulate, it becomes stagnant. Banks want you to stop the flow of your money so they can gain the motion of your money.

So the question is, how can you turn money from an *or* asset to an *and* asset, just like banks and wealthy people? We are almost there, but first, we need to discover "H.O.W." to be wealthy.

CHAPTER 6

H.O.W. to be Wealthy—Know Your Number Ones

We've already established that tax is your number one wealth destroyer. In this chapter, we are going to discuss your other number ones and how to design a financial model like that of the wealthy.

Number One Asset: Yourself

Recognize your number one asset. What's the number one asset that you will have throughout your lifetime? It's not your house, your car, or your career. It's *you!* You must realize that you are your number one asset. So, if you want to know where to put your money, invest in yourself.

If you can make yourself a better businessperson, a better real estate investor, a better boss, a better manager, or a better employee, that's the number one place to put your money. It's no secret that all top CEOs and business owners have business coaches. They're investing in themselves to make themselves better at what they do. Real estate investors have coaches, too—and that's not a secret, either. They invest in themselves to make themselves better at all aspects of real estate, from locating properties to arranging financing.

Whether you are spending money on education, mindset development, coaching, or the appropriate university degree to make yourself better, you need to recognize that you are your number one asset. There is no asset that you will ever have with nearly the same value to you as yourself. You are the golden goose.

Number One Investment: Business

Your number one investment is your business. If you own a business, it will always be your greatest investment. After you've invested in yourself, the next place to invest is in your business.

Statistics show that investing in your business consistently earns a higher return over time than you will ever earn in the stock market. After all, when you invest in the stock market, you are simply investing in other people's businesses.

Do you really know what management is doing at any given company? Do you know what product launches are coming out and if they will be successful? Can you predict which industries will be disrupted in the next five to ten years and make bets accordingly?

You must have a pretty good crystal ball if you can do all that! As the saying goes, the future is notoriously hard to predict. When you invest in other people's businesses via the stock market—whether you are choosing individual stocks, mutual funds, index funds, or whatever—you are betting on the other guy. You've got to learn to bet on yourself. If you manage your business successfully by investing in yourself and learning how to be the best possible business owner, you will be able to create returns that stock market investors can only dream of. Wealthy people know this. Middle-class people often do not.

Number One Way to Become a Millionaire: Real Estate

I am not telling you to run out and start a business or invest in real estate. What I am telling you is that over the past two hundred years, 90 percent of the world's millionaires have been created through real estate. What I am telling you is that if I, after having spent twenty-five years in the financial services industry, reflect on every single person of wealth that I have ever met, dealt with, lived by, known, or even had a colleague deal with, they all have done one of two things (though in some cases, both). They have either owned a business or invested in real estate. That's it. Full stop.

The strategies in Part Two of this book will help anyone who applies them become wealthier, regardless of whether or not he or she is a real estate investor or business owner. But if you want to become "wealthy, wealthy," investing in real estate and owning your own business are the keys to success.

Now let's look at this model and see why the typical financial plan will make it difficult for you to become wealthy. I call the model, the H.O.W. to be Wealthy model, or the Hierarchy of Wealth.

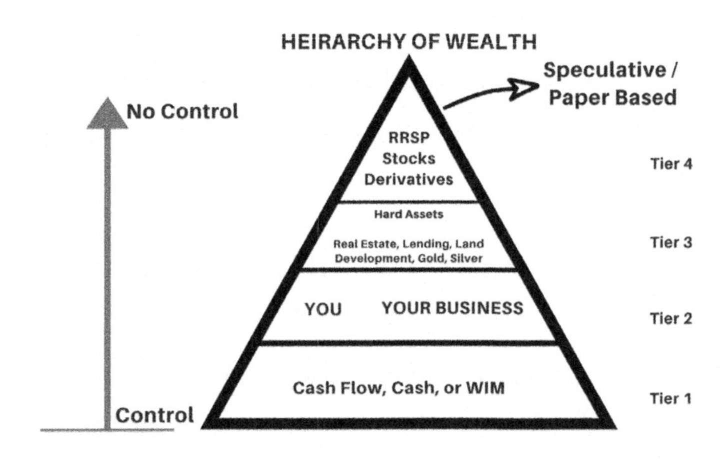

On the Hierarchy of Wealth, the base of the plan—the foundation, or Tier 1 money—must be cash flow, cash, or a Wealth and Income Maximization™ (WIM™) account. (I will later describe the WIM account and why it is your **number one strategy**, but let's stick with the model for now.)

At the base of your plan, you must be in control. You must be able to use and deploy dollars in Tier 1 to Tier 2 (investing in yourself and/or your business) and Tier 3 (investing in hard assets, such as real estate, private lending, land development, gold, and silver).

Tier 4 assets are the paper-based speculative stuff, like the stock market. Notice that as you move up the tiers, the amount of control you have decreases. If you know that to become wealthier, you need to invest in yourself, your business, and hard assets/real estate, then it is logical to start with Tier 1, building up your opportunity fund to deploy to those moneymakers.

However, typical financial planning tells us to go to school, graduate, and start saving right away in Tier 4. But there, we have no control. We cannot put anything into Tier 2 and/or Tier 3—where the real money is made—and let it sit there for the next forty or fifty years and hope it all works out. Does this make sense to you?

We need to have control over our money so we can take advantage of opportunities and deal with emergencies. If we have access to money, we will find opportunities.

Now, let's do a quick recap of Part One and move on to Part Two: what the wealthy do.

PART ONE WRAP-UP

10 Reasons the Deck Is Stacked Against You

Compare the wealthy to the middle class. They aren't necessarily smarter. Sometimes they aren't even more educated. So why are they able to achieve what the middle class can't achieve? It's because the deck is stacked against the middle class. Here are the ten most critical ways the deck is stacked against you, broken up into the two phases of Retirement Mountain.

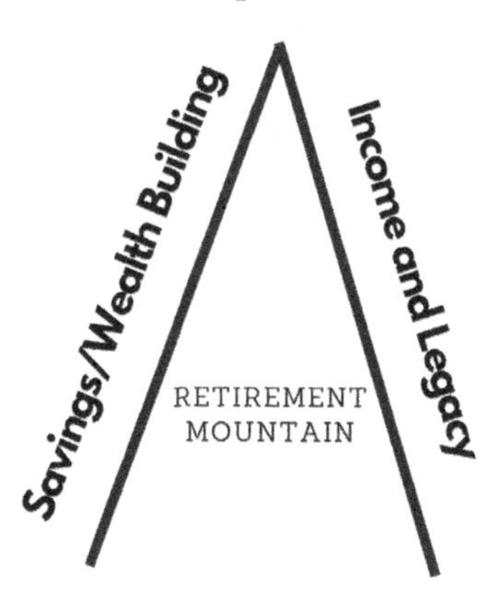

Phase 1: Savings and Wealth Building

1. No uninterrupted compounding. The wealthy are able to use their dollars without pulling them out of their investment vehicles.

2. *Or* assets instead of *and* assets. The wealthy can use their dollars for multiple things at once. The middle class needs to choose.

3. The four wealth destroyers. The wealthy have learned to tame major destroyers such as taxation, which members of the middle class frequently fall victim to.

4. No control. The wealthy put their money in assets they control so they can take advantage of opportunities and deal with emergencies.

5. Cannot use H.O.W. with current investments. Members of the middle class are rarely able to create a complete Hierarchy of Wealth due to their resources being incorrectly allocated.

6. Savings. Separating dollars into short-term (banking) and long-term (stock market) savings isn't a recipe for success.

7. No opportunity or emergency fund. When an opportunity or an emergency occurs, members of the middle class cannot access money because they aren't in control of it.

Phase 2: Income and Legacy

8. Horrible investments to generate income. Members of the middle class are relegated to either interest or the Monte Carlo method of preserving their passive income.

9. Pressure is on the rate of return. Members of the middle class are dependent on a single economic power, the rate of return, to yield their results. They're betting on a single element.

10. Retirement risks. For the most part, many people have done nothing to reduce or eliminate their retirement risks. This will become problematic as they start going down Retirement Mountain.

I didn't add *legacy* to the list because it is not a big concern for some people when they are saving or building wealth. However, I can tell you that your views may change as you become wealthier and older. And when these views change, you will realize typical financial planning does a poor job for legacy as well.

Those are the ten reasons that the deck is stacked against you, and that concludes Part One—why the middle class does not become wealthy. But now we're going to enter into Part Two, and discover what members of the middle class *can* do to start building their wealth and their retirement.

PART TWO

CHAPTER 7

Be the Bank!!—The WIM™ Account

In the last pages of Part One, we identified the top ten reasons the middle class does not become wealthy. So the solution that the wealthy have been employing simply needs to overcome all these reasons. The good news is that there is a solution that does all these things—plus a whole lot more.

It's been around for over one hundred years, and it will allow you to achieve uninterrupted compounding for the rest of your life. You will be in control of your dollars and be able to use your dollars as an *and* asset. It will slay the wealth destroyers, and allow you to invest in yourself, your business, and real estate. It's the perfect opportunity/emergency fund, and a place that you can put short-term and long-term dollars.

Then, when you reach the top of Retirement Mountain, and it's time to take an income, even if you've never started a business or invested in real estate, you will have more money. You can double your income, reduce risks, and still leave a legacy!

Sound good?

What's this miraculous solution? It's a *specially designed, dividend-paying, high-cash-value life insurance contract with a mutual company or participating whole life fund.*

That is a mouthful. I can shorten it to "high cash value life insurance" for now. I will even shorten it more later. The goal with this product is to grow our cash tax-free. Think of it like you would starting your own tax-free bank. Now you can operate like a bank and have your money do multiple jobs.

High-cash-value life insurance is like no other insurance product. It's very seldom seen—and the way we design it makes it even more rare. Because it is still a life insurance contract, it does come with some death benefit. But our focus is the cash value. Our goal is to **maximize the cash value** and **minimize the death benefit**.

Before you drop your jaw and say, "Life insurance!?" remember that it is a unique approach with a unique product. Also, this is exactly what the banks in North America use. Several banks have over $20 billion in high-cash-value life insurance.

The below chart lists US banks and how many billions—with a B—that they have of this specialty product. The Canadian banks operating in the United States have to disclose the cash value they have invested in their US operations inside of life insurance policies. Even though these Canadian banks have only been operating in the US for a relatively short period of time, some already have billions inside this product.

Remember, we want to act like a bank. There is a reason they put their money inside a tax-free compound machine.

Bank	Total Tier 1 Capital 12/31/16 $$/Billions	Holdings Life Ins/CSV 12/31/16 $$/Billions
Bank of America	$149.76	$21.48
JP Morgan Chase	$179.34	$10.10
Wells Fargo	$132.23	$18.30
U.S. Bank	$37.11	$5.75
BNY Mellon	$19.01	$4.03
PNC Bank	$29.50	$8.04
KeyBank	$12.44	$3.86

Canadian Banks in USA	Life Insurance CSV in $US
BMO Harris	$3.023 Billion
RBC	$1.673 Billion

Walt Disney used his policy to build Disneyland when the banks laughed at his amusement park idea.

Ray Kroc used it to grow McDonald's.

Ted Rogers used it to grow Rogers Communications in Canada.

Fewer than one-quarter of 1 percent of life insurance policies sold in Canada are designed this way. Within a policy, cash value grows tax-free. You can access it tax-free, and it is paid tax-free at death.

As one of my mentors explained to me, the rich don't care what it's called, they just love what it does. In Canada last year, approximately $1 billion was deposited into whole life insurance.

So, let's look at participating whole life to see what it is, what it does, and why we want it.

When we look at the number of insurance companies in Canada, and we multiply that by how many different insurance products they offer, our options get into thousands of eligible insurance products to choose from. However, when we narrow it down to how many mutual companies and participating whole life options we have to choose from, that meet our requirements, that number is down to four products.

Four products out of thousands—told you it was rare.

Each of the participating whole life funds we deal with has been around for over one hundred years. They have all paid a dividend each and every year—through the Depression, the world wars, the stock market crashes, etc. There is no reverse gear in these funds. Once you have $50,000 of cash value (or any amount), you can never go backward, like with the stock market. You will become wealthier each and every year.

Let's look at the last 25 years of dividends to see what the dividend history has been. This dividend chart is a blend of several companies.

Dividend Scale Historical Performance

Year	Whole Life Dividend Scale Interest Rate	S&P/TSX total return	Five-Year GIC
1995	10.0%	14.5%	7.9%
1996	9.6%	28.3%	6.9%
1997	9.8%	15.0%	5.9%
1998	9.4%	-1.6%	5.3%
1999	9.0%	31.7%	5.6%
2000	8.8%	7.4%	6.0%
2001	8.8%	-12.6%	5.3%
2002	8.7%	-12.4%	5.1%
2003	8.5%	26.7%	4.5%
2004	8.3%	14.5%	4.3%
2005	8.2%	24.1%	3.9%
2006	8.0%	17.3%	4.2%
2007	7.9%	9.8%	4.3%
2008	7.9%	-33.0%	3.4%
2009	7.3%	35.1%	2.8%
2010	7.1%	17.6%	2.9%
2011	7.1%	-8.7%	2.5%
2012	7.0%	7.2%	1.6%
2013	7.1%	13.0%	2.0%
2014	7.1%	10.6%	1.9%
2015	6.8%	-8.3%	1.2%
2016	6.7%	21.1%	1.0%
2017	6.5%	9.1%	1.6%
2018	6.4%	-8.9%	2.2%
2019	6.2%	22.9%	1.5%
25 Year Average	7.9%	8.3%	3.1%
Standard Deviation	1.0%	16.4%	1.5%

The dividend rate for the past twenty-five years has been 6, 7, 8, and even 9 percent and higher. What happened in 2008, when markets tumbled? Paid a dividend of 7.9 percent. What about the bumpy period from 2000 to 2002? Again, a dividend of around 8 percent.

It is uncorrelated to the stock market. Remember the wealth destroyer volatility? Standard deviation measures the volatility of an investment. The participating whole life fund had a standard deviation of around 1 percent versus the stock market of about 16.5 percent over the same period.

Volatility is what the Average vs. Actual Rate of Return example illustrated. We haven't eliminated it, but we've come pretty close. We have tamed the wealth destroyer volatility.

Mutual Companies and Participating Whole Life

When you deal with an experienced high-cash-value or Infinite Banking Authorized Practitioner, they will explain to you the advantages of a mutual company and/or a participating whole life fund. They have very similar characteristics.

A mutual company is an insurance company that is owned by the whole life policyholders. A participating whole life fund is not a company. It is owned by the policyholders.

Let's take a look at participating whole life funds first.

A participating whole life fund is a fund that is owned by the policyholders. All the money in the fund (often upward of $10 billion, $12 billion, or even $30 billion) is owned by the whole life policyholders. Therefore, all the profits from the fund get distributed to the policyholders (less a small management fee).

So how were they able to get such consistent returns? How were they able to pay a dividend every year for over one hundred years? How was the participating whole life fund able to increase in value each and every year with no reverse gear? What kind of magical investments did they have?

Well, there's nothing magical about it. Let's dig in a little deeper. We are going to look at the five ways to win by owning a participating whole life contract. They will not explain the entire return—there are still tons of actuarial calculations that are done by the actuaries—but they will explain a lot of it.

First, let's look at the investments.

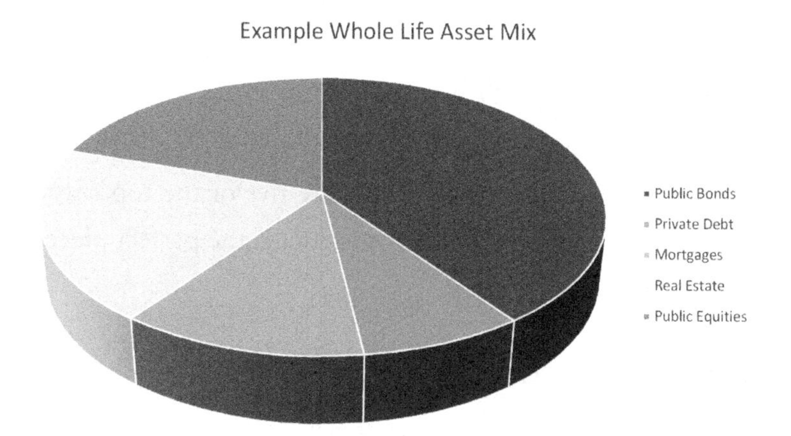

This is a typical makeup of a participating whole life fund: public bonds, private debt, mortgages, real estate, and a little bit in public equities or blue-chip stocks.

These investments are predominantly in interest rate–sensitive investments, and these investments have two very distinct differences to a typical bond fund or mutual fund. Remember the penny example? Tax-free, it grew to $10.7 million. At 50 percent tax, it grew to only $1,900 in thirty-one days. The whole life fund grows tax-free. Imagine a 5 percent bond growing tax-free for the next fifty years versus at 50 percent tax.

A second difference is the long-term investing approach. Most bond fund managers are interested in hitting their quarterly or annual targets to trigger a bonus or solicit more funds. The participating whole life fund managers are interested in having funds there in forty, fifty, or sixty years or more to pay future death claims, so they truly are investing for the long term, with long-term mortgages, bonds, etc.

The Five Ways to Win

We said there were five ways to win by purchasing a participating whole life contract. These are five of the top reasons why a participating whole life contract is the perfect place to save or store your money.

1. The Federal Government

The first way to win involves the federal government. This

is about the only time I ever want the federal government involved in my financial life. Years ago, the federal government began regulating what the insurance companies could charge for investment expenses for the participating whole life funds.

That's right. The insurance company is limited to what they can charge to manage the fund on the policyholder's behalf.

The investment expenses on the average mutual fund in Canada are 2.20 percent. For participating whole life accounts, the investment expenses average between 0.10 percent and 0.18 percent. The mutual fund charges twenty times the fees, versus the participating whole life investment management expense.

Wow! That's a huge difference.

2. Mortality Gains (or Longevity Gains)

Imagine you manage a participating whole life fund, and a forty-year-old buys a policy with a $100,000 death benefit. Your life tables tell you he is going to die at sixty-seven. What do you do next?

Well, you would figure out that you need to charge some number per month—let's say, $300—to be able to pay that claim. This is simplified, but it's the core of how actuarial calculations are made.

Now suppose that man lived to be eighty-seven years old before he died—twenty more years than expected—before he collected the $100,000. Your fund collected an extra $300 per month for an extra 240 months, or an extra $72,000.

Life expectancy in Canada is continuing to increase year over year, decade over decade. So, as people start living longer, the mortality gains get released back to the participating whole life fund and distributed to the policyholders. For all the thousands of insurance products out there besides participating whole life (and mutual companies), those extra profits go back to the insurance company.

3. Cancellations

There are many, many, *many* poorly designed insurance contracts out there. Sometimes, if you cancel your policy in the first few years, or even the first five years, there's almost no cash value returned to you. In these circumstances, all that money from cancellation goes back into the participating whole life fund and gets distributed to the policyholders.

4. Expenses and Taxes

Actuaries conservatively price these contracts for years, and expenses and taxes are consistently estimated at a higher number than what the actual expenses and taxes are.

An insurance company twenty years ago likely had two floors of super computers in their head office to calculate actuarial calculations. Now they could probably do it on a phone app. So these "expense and tax gains" again get released back into the whole life fund and out to the policyholders.

5. Investment Returns

Investment returns make up the fifth way that the participating whole life fund is able to produce those consistent, boring, effective, tax-free dividends year after year after year. As we saw earlier, the fund invests in safe, long-term investments.

Those are the superb benefits of a participating whole life fund.

If you understand a participating whole life fund, a mutual company is easy to understand. With a mutual company, the whole life policyholders own the whole life fund *and* the rest of the company as well. They benefit from the profit of *all* the lines of business that the company is involved in.

The Wealth and Income Maximization Account

In the first chapter, we talked about the two distinct phases of Retirement Mountain:

- Wealth Building and Saving (climbing the mountain)
- Income and Legacy (going down the mountain)

We now know the solution to this, but it can be hard to talk about—fundamentally so, because the name is a mouthful! Instead of calling it a "high-cash-value, specially designed, dividend-paying whole life contract with a participating fund or a mutual company," I've developed a much-easier-to-say name.

The name I use with my clients is representative of what it does: *Wealth and Income Maximization (WIM) account.*

It is the perfect account in which to save money and maximize wealth. It is the perfect vehicle to maximize both retirement income and legacy—both sides of the mountain. (We will be reviewing how to accomplish these goals in the remaining chapters.)

For now, let's look at an example of a typical policy. You can set up a policy with a monthly deposit, an annual deposit, a lump sum, or a combination of all of these.

Notice I call it a *deposit,* not a *premium.* Once I pay my car insurance premium or house insurance premium, the money is gone. However, if I have $40,000 in Bank A, and I move $20,000 to Bank B, I still have $40,000; it is just deposited somewhere else. Think of the WIM account as your own bank. You could pay for longer or shorter than twenty years—you could pay for three years, five years, or sixty years.

The first year of a high-cash-value life insurance contract is a lot like starting a business. You are capitalizing or investing in the business, and you are usually not up money. So if your goal is to cancel the policy after one year, this is a no-good, rotten idea and you should run away now.

However, if your goal is to compound tax-free for the rest of your life, be in control of your money, multiply your money without risk, maximize your wealth and income, then continue reading. This is for you.

In year one of a typical WIM policy, you typically have a cash value between 60 and 70 percent of the amount deposited. Told you the first year was not good. However, after a few years, your cash value will grow somewhere between 3.5 percent and 5.5 percent tax-free for life, depending on a number of factors, including health.

Imagine if your savings plan could grow tax-free and not be affected by the wealth destroyers for the rest of your life; the difference is worth millions.

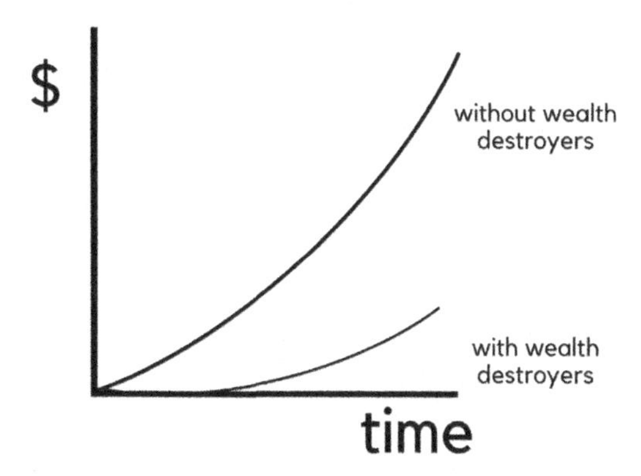

It's true that 3.5 percent to 5.5 percent tax-free is a very competitive rate of return, but it's not the most important point at all. The most important point is that now you are in control of your money. You can access 90 percent of the cash value at any time with just a phone call. You could access $40,000 in year three for a vehicle purchase or to deal with an emergency. You could access $80,000 in year five to take advantage of an amazing opportunity, or $300,000 in year thirteen to buy a business or apartment building and plan an amazing vacation.

You could access the cash value thirty-seven times or more, and your cash value would not be affected at all. This is because you are not *cashing out* your cash value to use the money. You are borrowing against the cash value. Your money inside the policy continues to grow uninterrupted for life!

Your compound snowball continues to grow until the day you die. The death benefit will continue to grow each year as well, and will be higher than the cash value until age one hundred, when they meet.

Just think of the power of having your own bank! In your WIM account, your money will grow 4 percent to 5 percent tax-free every year, *and* you will be able to use the money at the same time outside the policy.

How many more opportunities could you take advantage of? How many financial emergencies or expenses could you deal with, without affecting your long-term growth?

This brings me to the money multiplier. Your money is inside the policy, working for you (growing). It can also be outside the policy (loan against policy), working for you at the same time. Here is an example with a 90 percent loan.

Money Multiplier at Various Years

Total Deposit	Money Inside Policy Working for You	Money Outside Policy Working for You	Total Money Working for You	As a Percentage of Deposits
$60,000	$50,000	$45,000	$95,000	158%
$400,000	$600,000	$540,000	$1,140,000	285%

Even in the early years, where total deposits ($60,000) exceed cash value ($50,000), when you combine that with the potential amount outside of policy working for you, you have 158 percent of deposits working for you.

After the policy has been in force for a while and the cash exceeds deposits, you now have 285 percent of deposits working for you. This is what the rich do. This is what banks do. They take one dollar and make it do more.

The WIM account, first and foremost, is the perfect spot in which to save or store money. You can save money inside the WIM account in a systematic way (every month), or transfer large amounts from other savings/investments—the same thing the bank does.

Below, I want to show you the benefits of the WIM account as a savings plan, or place to warehouse wealth. We are going to compare short-term and long-term savings.

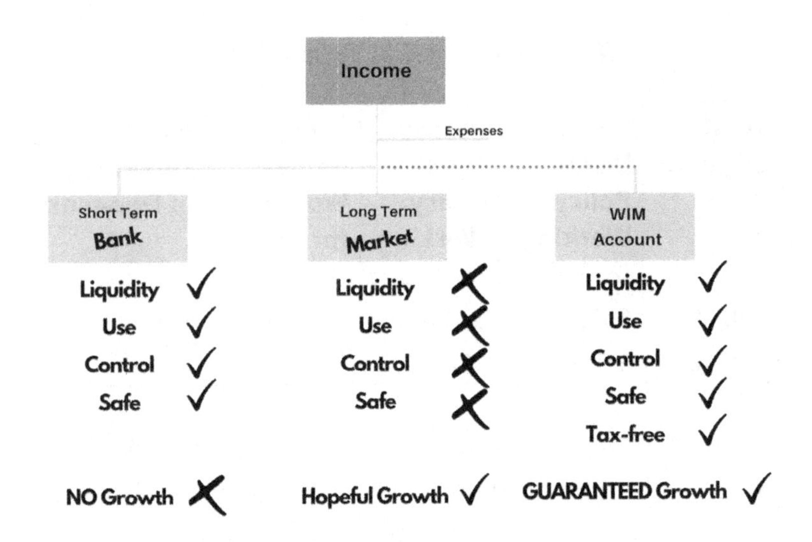

This is how most people save. They take their income—minus their expenses—and then deposit their short-term savings in a bank. Why? Because they may need the money in the short term, and they do not want to lose it. The bank offers them liquidity, use, control, and safety. What they give up in return is growth.

For long-term savings, most people choose the stock market. They give up liquidity, use, control, and safety in exchange for "hopeful growth."

With the WIM account, you enjoy all of the benefits of short-term and long-term savings plus tax-free growth, death benefit, and more.

See now why Bank of America has over $20 billion of this type of cash-value life insurance?

Let's briefly revisit the wealth destroyers, starting with Interrupting Compound Interest.

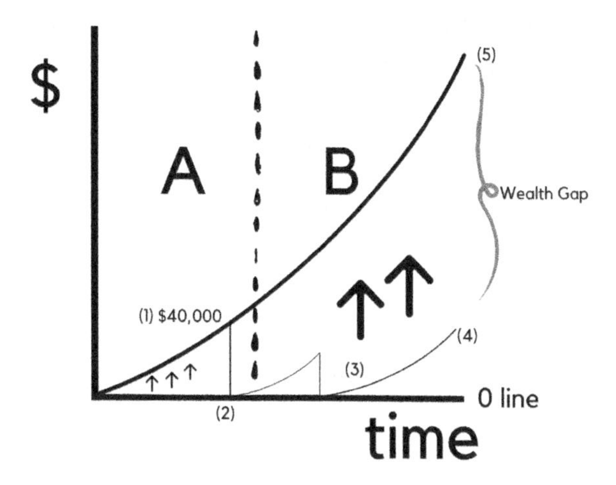

The above was the slide from Part One, where we saw what happens when someone pays cash or interrupts the compounding. There is a huge wealth gap compared to where the wealthy, banks, big corporations, and people who know about this concept end up.

Let's see how the WIM account can eliminate this wealth gap for you.

Imagine you have $50,000 inside your WIM account, and you need $40,000 for an opportunity or an expense. Instead of cashing out your account, you simply use the insurance company's money. You call our office or the insurance company directly and tell them to deposit $40,000 into your account.

Why would you want to use the insurance company's money?

If you do, your money inside the policy can continue to grow *uninterrupted.* It can grow to $100,000, $200,000, $400,000, $2 million, $4 million, and beyond. You can compound for life, just like the wealthy.

OK, so it makes sense from your side. Of course you want to use the insurance company's money! But why would they let you?

Here are the top four reasons:

- Contractual Obligation
- Perfect Risk
- Death
- Interest

First, they are contractually obligated to loan you 90 percent of the cash value of your account. That's *your* money. They do not ask what the loan is for, when or how you are going to pay it back, or anything else. They just deposit it in your account.

Second, you are the perfect risk. When a financial institution loans money against a property, there is a risk. What if the property goes down in value, gets destroyed, or something else? Then they have to foreclose on it, fix it, and try to resell it.

Compare this to the cash value inside the policy. It is guaranteed not to go backward. It is guaranteed to go up each year and can be accessed like cash—the perfect risk.

Now, in the event of death, the insurance company is even more protected. The death benefit is always higher than the cash value (and equal at age one hundred). In the unlikely event you die the day after you take out the $40,000 loan against the policy, the death benefit will be paid minus the outstanding loan.

If the death benefit was $500,000, your loved ones get a cheque for $500,000 minus the loan of $40,000—or $460,000, tax-free.

And finally, the insurance company will charge you interest. The amount of interest varies between companies, but let's use 5 percent for this example. Is this a good interest rate? For the type of loan it is, it is an incredible interest rate.

This type of loan is called an unstructured loan. An unstructured loan means you pay back the loan when you want, how you want, and if you want.

Imagine you borrow $40,000 to buy a car or an income property. You decide to pay back $2,000 per month. But, ten months in, something bad happens financially. Maybe the roof blows off the house, you become temporarily disabled, or you lose your job. Imagine calling up the bank and asking if you can stop paying those car payments or mortgage payments for a while, or longer.

With a WIM account, you can simply decide to stop making payments immediately for the next six, twelve, or eighteen months, or longer. It's your money.

Even better, you can say, "Remember that $20,000 I paid toward my loan in the last ten months? I need that back. And the $4,000 to $5,000 my policy grew in the past ten months? I want that too. Stop my payments, and deposit $25,000 into my account."

You are now in *control.* You are not beholden to the whims of the bank. *You are the bank.*

The wealth destroyer Interrupting Compound Interest has been eliminated.

Taxes: The money inside the WIM account grows tax-free, can be accessed tax-free, and is tax-free at death. Wealth destroyer eliminated.

Fees: The WIM account investment expense is 0.1 percent to 0.18 percent. Wealth destroyer severely tamed.

Volatility: The standard deviation on a WIM account is 1 percent versus the stock market's volatility, at 16 percent. Wealth destroyer severely tamed.

Remember what happened to the penny when it grew without the wealth destroyers? We can't achieve a 100 percent return a day, but you can picture the impact when we slay the wealth destroyers using the WIM account.

To learn even more about becoming the bank, I suggest you read the book *Becoming Your Own Banker* by R. Nelson

Nash. Then read it again and again through the years. You will learn something new each time.

CHAPTER 8

How to Control AND Compound Your Money Forever

The following three words are the ones I use the most often when describing financial success to clients. If you want to be wealthy, or wealthier than you are today, eliminate the wealth destroyers in your financial life, and follow these three words: ***control and compound***.

Control

With the WIM account, you are in control. You can access money when you want. Need money ASAP to close a deal? Done. Don't want to try to explain to the bank why you need the money? No problem, you are the bank. If the stock market or real estate market drops 50 percent and you want cash to take advantage of opportunities, it's done. Lose your job or have an expense? Easy.

You can pay it back when you want, how you want, and *if* you want. Want to do a real estate flip and make no payments for twelve months—sure, no problem. Want to pay the loan back $1,000 per month and then make one large lump sum payment? Again, no problem. Want to borrow to invest or start a business and make no payments until investment starts growing? Yes, yes, yes.

Remember, if you are the bank, you get to decide if you should get the loan, and you decide how you should pay it back.

The <u>And</u> Asset

Once you deposit money into your WIM account—boom, you have compounding for the rest of your life. You also have

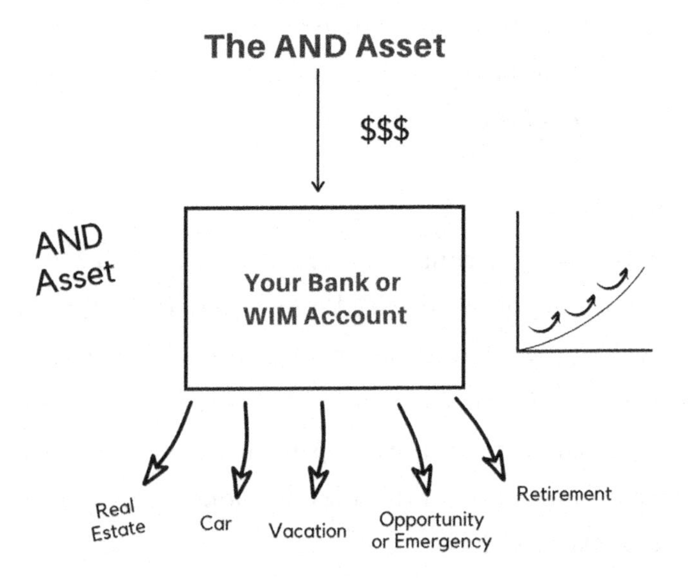

an *and* asset. The WIM account allows your money to grow inside the account tax-free, *and* you can use that money for real estate *and* buying a car *and* vacations *and* a business opportunity *and* emergencies *and* retirement.

Compound

Albert Einstein said, "Compound interest is the eighth wonder of the world. He who understands it, earns it; he who doesn't, pays it."

The banks, the wealthy, and the big corporations have understood this forever. Now it's your turn. Most people stop compounding by interrupting the compound curve, paying taxes and fees, and suffering volatility.

Furthermore, when people reach retirement, they start depleting their savings (stopping their compounding) until their balances drop to $0. With the WIM account, you will compound until the day you die.

Here is the difference between compounding for five years and fifty.

Current Value	If You Compound for Five Years	If You Compound for 50 Years
$100,000	$127,628	$1.15 million

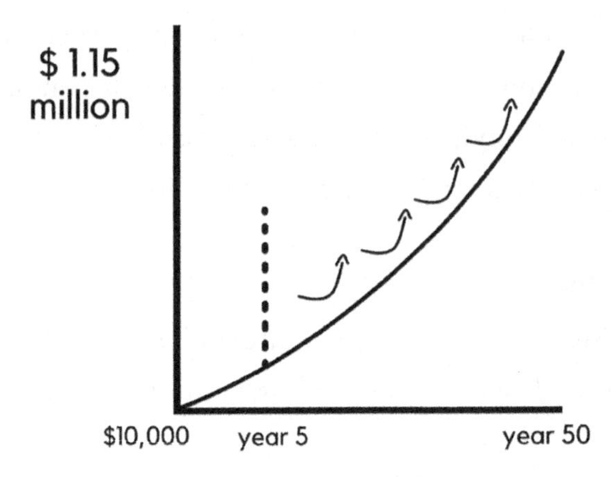

Now that we know the WIM account will eliminate the wealth destroyers, grow tax-free at 3.5 percent to 5.5 percent, and allow us to ***control and compound***, let's revisit the Hierarchy of Wealth.

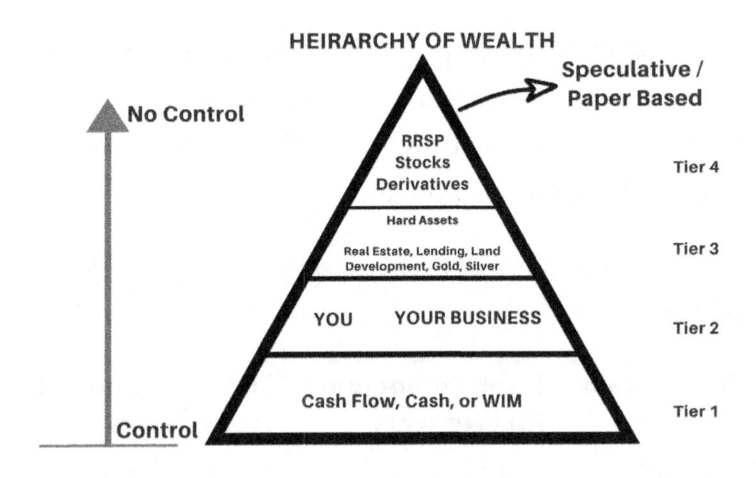

Tier 1, or the base of a properly built financial strategy has to have a place where you are in control. The previous chapters have pointed out how the WIM account is far superior to cash.

Save or transfer your money to the WIM account, and then you are in control. You can invest in yourself, your business, or hard assets—or just deal with your expenses.

An interesting exercise is to lay out all your assets on one sheet of paper. Circle in red all the ones that are taxable or tax-deferred (RRSPs). Then circle in green all the ones that are tax-free and you have true control over (even if the market crashes). A lot of people get stuck on the first step.

Next, which of the assets circled in green will compound for life? And, finally, which ones are *and* assets, in which ones are *and* assets that you can keep growing tax-free and use somewhere else as well?

CHAPTER 9

WIM Account for Real Estate Investors

The Wealth and Income Maximization account is a perfect fit for real estate investors and business owners. Both of these groups need to store cash, need to be in control of their money, need easy and quick access to their money, and already feel they pay enough tax. They want maximum flexibility on their deposits and repayment terms, and they realize their best investment is going to be their business and/or real estate. They can't have their money in jail; they need to be able to deploy it at any time into a business or real estate transaction—or even for day-to-day expenses.

Real estate investors understand the importance of their dollar doing more than one job. If we look at typical financial planning, where you invest in the stock market, your money hopefully does one job: it appreciates. The stock or fund you own is in the casino of Wall Street, and you hope it goes up.

That's it—one hopeful job.

Now let's look at rental real estate and the different jobs the same dollar can do.

Passive Appreciation	Tax Benefits
Active Appreciation	Principle Repayment
Positive Cash Flow	Leverage

When you invest a dollar into a rental property, it can have passive appreciation; it increases in value. You can also have active appreciation; you can do a renovation or improve the property to increase its value and earning potential.

Purchased correctly, you can have positive cash flow every month. Your rental income is higher than your expenses. Tax benefits include writing off depreciation and your interest expense deduction.

Principle repayment is when the tenants are basically paying down your mortgage for you; each year, your mortgage balance shrinks, and your net worth goes up.

And, finally, there is perhaps the biggest job a dollar can do with real estate: the power of leverage. Experienced real estate investors know that leverage can be one of the largest wealth-building strategies around.

If you buy a rental unit for $100,000 and it goes up $10,000 in value, how much will you make on appreciation? If you pay cash, you will make 10 percent on appreciation ($10,000 ÷ $100,000 = 10 percent).

But what if you only put a 20 percent down payment on the property? Will it still appreciate the same amount even if you have a mortgage? Of course it will. Now, the money you'll make on the appreciation is 50 percent ($10,000 growth ÷ $20,000 deposit = 50 percent). When you use a 20 percent down payment, your appreciation is multiplied five times because of the power of leverage.

If we add up these benefits, they may look like this in one year:

Passive Appreciation:	2%	
Active Appreciation:	0%	no renovation
Positive Cash Flow:	8%	
Tax Benefits:	5%	
Principle Repayment:	9%	
Leverage:	10%	

You can see why real estate investing has created so many millionaires. But what about a bad year? What if the market is flat and there is no appreciation at all?

You will lose the passive appreciation that year, as well as the five times multiplier of leverage, but guess what? Because your dollar is doing more than one job, you're still making money. This is a powerful strategy.

Now let's combine this powerful strategy with the other powerful strategy we learned about: the WIM account.

What happens if you put your cash inside the WIM account first, and then borrow it to use it for real estate?

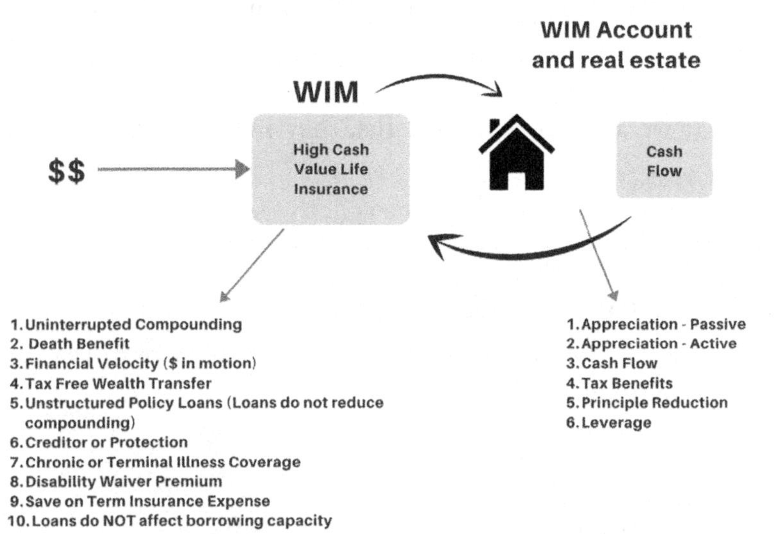

You deposit money into the WIM account, and then you borrow the money to purchase the real estate. With the WIM account, you now have uninterrupted compounding for the rest of your life.

It also comes with a death benefit. You achieve financial velocity (money in motion, like the banks). It can result in a tax-free transfer at death. And it gives you the power of unstructured loans—a real estate investor's dream.

It can also provide creditor protection (personal polices). In the event you go bankrupt or get sued, your money can be protected.

And what about life's most unexpected events? It comes with built-in Chronic or Terminal Illness coverage that can pay up to 25 percent of the death benefit for one more trip around the world if you are terminally ill. If you purchase the disability waiver and become disabled, the insurance will pay your deposits for the rest of the contract! Ask your bank, if you become disabled, if they would mind contributing to your savings plan every month for the next twenty to forty years.

And although our focus with the WIM account is cash value, it does come with a death benefit much larger than the cash value. You may be able to save thousands by terminating some term insurance you no longer need, because you will have a death benefit with this product (however, never cancel any insurance without a review from a licensed professional).

Finally, the real estate investor's favorite—loans do not affect borrowing capacity. Here is an example of that in action. Imagine you have an amazing opportunity to buy a cash-flowing $600,000 building. The appraisal comes in good, and the bank says they will loan you 80 percent of the $600,000 ($480,000), in a traditional mortgage, if you can come up with a 20 percent down payment ($120,000).

Can you take that money from your RRSP or pension? No, that money is in jail. Can you take that money from your kids' RESP? No, that money is in jail. What if your TFSA or market-based investments are down 50 percent after a big drop in the market; would you access the money and lock in losses?

If you tell the bank that you are going to borrow the money against your personal home equity line of credit, they will not grant you the 80 percent mortgage because you will be financing 100 percent of the purchase price. If you say you'll take out a personal loan, same answer.

However, if you borrow against your WIM account, the bank will not consider that a loan for borrowing purposes. In effect, you will be using $480,000 of the bank's money and $120,000 of the insurance company's money to purchase property. Remember, you are not cashing out your WIM account. It is growing uninterrupted until the day you die.

You are using the insurance company's money with the WIM account as collateral.

You do this, the positive cash flow pays off the loan against the WIM account, and now you have *even more* positive cash flow.

What is the percentage return when you have a positive cash flow and you put $0 of your own money down? I'll give you a hint: think of the number 8 on its side.

So back to the now sixteen possible jobs your dollar can do when we combine the WIM account with real estate investing. You will never do all sixteen jobs in the same year. But if you can have your same dollar doing five or six jobs at the same time versus the "hope strategy" of one job in the stock market, you can see how powerful this is.

Remember the "Rule of Seventy-Two" from high school? If you divide seventy-two by the interest rate, the calculation will tell you how many years it will take your money to double. If your one-job stock market earns 4 percent, it will take eighteen years for the money to double (72 ÷ 4 percent = 18 years). If your dollar can do more than one job at the same time and earn approximately 18 percent, it will only take four years to double (72 ÷ 18 percent = 4 years).

But what would $100,000 earning approximately 18 percent grow to be by the end of eighteen years? Two million dollars!

See the chart below, and pick which option you want.

$100,000 Deposit

Interest Rate	Year 4	Year 18
4%	$117,000	$200,000
18% (multiple jobs)	$200,000	$2 million

This is with just one property. Real estate investors know they can "rinse and repeat." Once the loan from the insurance company is paid off (or before) with the positive cash flow, now you can purchase a second property and have two positive cash flows paying off a single loan used for down payment—then three, four, etc. It doesn't take long for these loans to be paid off in a year or less when you have multiple properties.

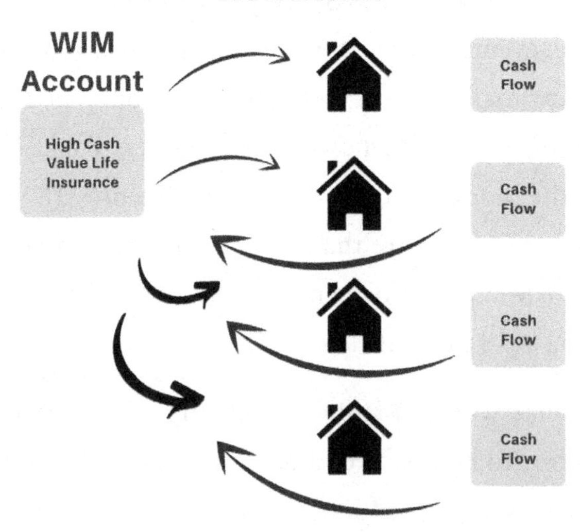

Now you have the perfect place to store your cash so you never have to pay tax on growth. You are operating as your own bank, and you are in control. Additionally, that death benefit that you were not as interested in when you started the WIM account may enable you to leave all the properties to your family, because you will receive a huge tax-free cheque right at the time you receive a big tax bill on these properties' growth—at death.

The WIM account is the perfect complementary product for real estate investors, which is one of the reasons why some of the largest policies sold in Canada are sold to real estate investors and their families.

CHAPTER 10

WIM Account for Business Owners

Whether or not you're a business owner, this chapter is going to be useful to you. Of course, it's also just a preview. Unfortunately, there isn't room in this book to do a complete review of this concept for business owners. There are only a handful of advisors in Canada who specialize in these concepts full-time; find an expert.

Remember, your family is your business. It has financial ups and downs, emergencies and opportunities. If you can run your family finances like a properly run business, your family will be much better off because of it.

Business owners tend to understand the WIM account very quickly because they understand the importance of cash flow.

Things can be going great in business, and, all of a sudden, you're not sure how you're going to make payroll. Almost all businesses are seasonal to some extent, and a business owner must decide what to do with his or her surplus cash in the busy times to make sure it is there in the lean times.

Sticking with cash flow, business owners also understand the importance of credit, or being able to access money when they need it. Banks tend to be more than willing to loan you money when you don't need it. But what about after a few bad quarters or years—or in 2008, when the market crashed—how easy was it to get money from banks at that time?

Since businesses know they need liquidity, surplus cash tends to sit in a bank account, earning a small amount and being taxed at over 50 percent. Business owners can't afford to put it in the market, in case of a market crash or a need for liquidity. Imagine you're at your next meeting with your team and your CFO, designing a perfect investment vehicle for this money. You stand at the whiteboard and ask for suggestions on designing this perfect savings/investment vehicle, and your team shouts out their ideas:

- Safe
- Liquid
- Tax-Free
- Cannot Lose
- No Volatility

- Guaranteed
- Competitive Rate of Return
- Unstructured Loans

I could list another ten characteristics, but you probably get the idea: the WIM account is the ideal spot for a business to store its cash. It is the ideal spot for the business to start acting like its own bank, so it is not beholden to its local bank.

The above references operating companies, but many business owners in Canada have holding companies. Let's use Jim Didwell as our example.

Jim owns a successful business and knows that for every dollar he pays out of the business to himself personally, he is going to pay about 50 percent tax and be left with fifty cents. He can pay this out as salary or pay a corporate tax rate of 11 to 12 percent inside the corporation and then give himself a dividend. Either way, he will net about fifty cents and pay 50 percent tax.

So, Jim, like many business owners in Canada, decides to leave some money inside the business. He pays the 11 to 12 percent small-business tax, and is left with approximately eighty-eight cents. We refer to these as *eighty-eight–cent dollars*—versus the *fifty-cent dollars* in the first scenario. Jim is pretty sharp and realizes if he can invest eighty-eight-cent dollars instead of fifty-cent dollars, he has 76 percent more money to invest.

These eighty-eight-cent dollars are dollars he does not need to run his business and are referred to as *retained earnings.*

Jim astutely moves these retained earnings into his holding company for several reasons, including reducing any exposure to creditors. Jim knows that he became wealthy by investing in himself, his business, and a few properties he bought that his business rents from him. So he wants to make sure he doesn't lose the money inside his holding company. He worked hard for it, and he never knows when or if he will ever need it.

Jim decides to put these retained earnings into a fixed-income portfolio mix of bonds, GICs, and money market funds. He thinks since he has already paid the small-business tax on this money (11 to 12 percent), he probably won't be taxed too badly on his money. Sadly, Jim realizes the taxes just keep coming. In fact, he faces three more levels of taxation:

- Taxes on Growth
- Taxes When He Spends it
- Taxes When He Dies

In every province in Canada, he will be taxed at approximately 50 percent on his growth! He will pay significant tax if he spends it, *and* he will face a large tax bill at death.

"I thought this was after-tax money!" he tells his CFO.

Fortunately, his CFO knows someone who specializes in this type of thing and calls him in.

Jim decides to transfer a part of his taxable investments inside his holding company to a corporate WIM account. He is able to eliminate or drastically reduce all three levels of taxation mentioned above.

He will be able to personally spend significantly more money (two to five times more) in retirement from the corporate WIM than he would have been able to from the taxable investment. He will also leave a significantly higher after-tax legacy to his family.

Tax is way down. His retirement income is way up. And his family receives way more. It's a true WIN, WIN, WIN with WIM!

CHAPTER 11

The WIM Account—Double Your Retirement Income and Reduce Your Retirement Risks

When we started this book, we discussed the concept of going up Retirement Mountain—the accumulation phase of life—and then coming down the other side, the retirement, spending, and giving-away portion of life.

My goal throughout the book has been to show you ways to enjoy more of your wealth. We've seen that wealthy people think and act like banks because they're able to enjoy the benefits of cash flow, the velocity of money, and having money perform multiple tasks.

Now that you're following these strategies, I'd like to discuss in this chapter how you can enjoy more of your wealth in retirement.

Coming down Retirement Mountain, as we've seen, people are rightly afraid to spend their money. They can either spend the interest or use the infamous Monte Carlo method, which allows them to spend just 3 to 3.5 percent of their savings, resulting in a cramped, unhappy lifestyle.

Let's talk about how our strategy gives you four economic powers that typical middle-class people do not enjoy:

- Rate of Return
- Actuarial Science
- Tax Diversification
- Uncorrelated Assets

Remember the retirement risks we discussed earlier:

Do you have enough money? Will the stock market crash in retirement? What will happen with interest rates and taxes? What about our health? Will my spouse or I need long-term care? How will inflation affect our spending power?

And then there's the biggest risk of all: longevity, the risk multiplier for all the others.

Now let's look at the wealthy person's strategy of being the bank, which can double your retirement income while reducing your risks. In order to do so, I'll show you five ways to spend your money more efficiently.

1. The Volatility Buffer

This strategy prevents you from taking money out of your investment portfolio in a down market. The WIM account is not correlated to the ups and downs of the stock market. In 2008, all the WIM accounts paid dividends between 7 and 8 percent. To see the impact of taking money out of a down market, consider what happened between 1970 and 1999. You may be saying, "Darren, that example is really dated!" But the numbers illustrate that even in the crazy heyday of the stock market, volatility will destroy your wealth. So let's use our Wayback Machine to see what happened half a century ago.

Actual Rates of Return 1970–1999

AVERAGE ROR:	**14.73%**		
	S&P 500 with Dividends		
Year			
1970	3.48	1985	31.16
1971	14.12	1986	18.59
1972	18.74	1987	5.78
1973	-14.42	1988	16.54
1974	-25.95	1989	31.44
1975	36.9	1990	-3.07
1976	23.72	1991	29.98
1977	-7.03	1992	7.48
1978	6.59	1993	9.98
1979	18.53	1994	1.32
1980	31.65	1995	37.2

1981	-4.64	1996	22.7
1982	20.38	1997	33.12
1983	22.33	1998	28.38
1984	6.08	1999	20.87

The average rate of return over this period was 14.73 percent. Wouldn't that be nice? Do you think your retirement would be easy if you could average a 14.73 percent return?

Let's say you retired in 1970 with $1 million, and you wanted to spend $100,000 a year in retirement. What would have happened? You took out $100,000—10 percent of your portfolio— in the first year. But you earned 14.73 percent on your money, so your account value actually went up. By the time you reached the age of seventy, you had almost $1.3 million in your account . . . and you were still taking out $100,000 each year.

Volatility Buffer with Average Returns

Year	Beg. Of Year Acct. Value	Earnings Rate	Spending Per Year	Growth	End of Year Acct. Value
1970	$1,000,000	14.73%	-$100,000	$132,570	$1,032,570
1971	$1,032,570	14.73%	-$100,000	$137,368	$1,069,938
1972	$1,069,938	14.73%	-$100,000	$142,872	$1,112,809
1973	$1,112,809	14.73%	-$100,000	$149,187	$1,161,996
1974	$1,161,996	14.73%	-$100,000	$156,432	$1,218,428
1975	$1,218,428	14.73%	-$100,000	$164,744	$1,283,173
1976	$1,283,173	14.73%	-$100,000	$174,281	$1,357,454
1977	$1,357,454	14.73%	-$100,000	$185,223	$1,442,677
1978	$1,442,677	14.73%	-$100,000	$197,776	$1,540,453
1979	$1,540,453	14.73%	-$100,000	$212,179	$1,652,632
1980	$1,652,632	14.73%	-$100,000	$228,703	$1,781,335
1981	$1,781,335	14.73%	-$100,000	$247,661	$1,928,995
1982	$1,928,995	14.73%	-$100,000	$269,411	$2,098,406
1983	$2,098,406	14.73%	-$100,000	$294,365	$2,292,772
1984	$2,292,772	14.73%	-$100,000	$322,995	$2,515,767

Year	Beg. Of Year Acct. Value	Earnings Rate	Spending Per Year	Growth	End of Year Acct. Value
1985	$2,515,767	14.73%	-$100,000	$355,842	$2,771,610
1986	$2,771,610	14.73%	-$100,000	$393,528	$3,065,138
1987	$3,065,138	14.73%	-$100,000	$436,765	$3,401,902
1988	$3,401,902	14.73%	-$100,000	$486,370	$3,788,273
1989	$3,788,273	14.73%	-$100,000	$543,283	$4,231,555
1990	$4,231,555	14.73%	-$100,000	$608,578	$4,740,133
1991	$4,740,133	14.73%	-$100,000	$683,492	$5,323,625
1992	$5,323,625	14.73%	-$100,000	$769,440	$5,993,065
1993	$5,993,065	14.73%	-$100,000	$868,048	$6,761,113
1994	$6,761,113	14.73%	-$100,000	$981,182	$7,642,295
1995	$7,642,295	14.73%	-$100,000	$1,110,980	$8,653,275
1996	$8,653,275	14.73%	-$100,000	$1,259,897	$9,813,173
1997	$9,813,173	14.73%	-$100,000	$1,430,750	$11,143,923
1998	$11,143,923	14.73%	-$100,000	$1,626,770	$12,670,693
1999	$12,670,693	14.73%	-$100,000	$1,851,663	*$14,422,356*

Do you think you had a stressful retirement? Do you think you were worried about the markets each and every day? Do you think you were worried about the retirement risks we've discussed?

Absolutely not! Instead, you had zero stress and a highly enjoyable retirement. By the thirtieth year, at $100,000 a year, you would have spent $3 million—and your account would have ballooned to over $14 million, which you would leave to your family.

Sounds blissful, right? You want this; am I correct?

Unfortunately, this whole thing is a myth. It never happened. Remember when we talked about average versus actual returns? The numbers we're talking about here relate to average returns. But it's actual returns we have to look at. Now let's use the only numbers that matter: the actual returns.

Volatility Buffer with ACTUAL Returns

Year	Beg. Of Year Acct. Value	Earnings Rate	Spending Per Year	Growth	End of Year Acct. Value
1970	$1,000,000	3.48%	-$100,000	$31,284	$931,284
1971	$931,284	14.12%	-$100,000	$117,363	$948,647
1972	$948,647	18.74%	-$100,000	$159,023	$1,007,670
1973	$1,007,670	-14.42%	-$100,000	-$130,864	$776,805
1974	$776,805	-25.95%	-$100,000	-$175,602	$501,204
1975	$501,204	36.90%	-$100,000	$148,052	$549,256
1976	$549,256	23.72%	-$100,000	$106,548	$555,804
1977	$555,804	-7.03%	-$100,000	-$32,024	$423,780
1978	$423,780	6.59%	-$100,000	$21,347	$345,127
1979	$345,127	18.53%	-$100,000	$45,424	$290,551
1980	$290,551	31.65%	-$100,000	$60,304	$250,855
1981	$250,855	-4.64%	-$100,000	-$7,000	$143,854
1982	$143,854	20.38%	-$100,000	$8,935	$52,790
1983	$52,790	22.33%	-$100,000	-$10,544	-$57,754

In the chart above, you started with $1 million in 1970, and still had $1 million at the start of 1973, but by 1975, it was down to half a million dollars. You lost half your capital in a two-year period because you took money out in a down market. Was this a stress-free retirement? No.

If you'd then continued on this path, based on actual return instead of average return, you would have been broke by the time you reached seventy-eight, and you would've had to ask your children to support you. Some people ask, why take money out in a down market? My response is, most of my clients who have retired still like to eat and sleep indoors!

So instead of leaving $14 million to your loved ones after a wealthy and comfortable retirement, you're out of money at age seventy-eight.

That's not what we want for you.

So what's the answer? The volatility buffer—which means you never take money out of the market after a negative year. You take it out only if the market has gone up. The smart alternative is to access income from your cash-value life insurance after a negative year on the market. If you'd done that only three times in our 1970–1999 scenario, you could have taken $100,000 out for the remaining thirty years, not run out of money, and left $2 million behind. That's twice what you started with, even though you spent $100,000 per year over the thirty years.

Volatility Buffer with WIM Account (Uncorrelated Asset)

Year	Beg. Of Year Acct. Value	Earnings Rate	Spending Per Year	Growth	End of Year Acct. Value
1970	$1,000,000	3.48%	-$100,000	$31,284	$931,284
1971	$931,284	14.12%	-$100,000	$117,363	$948,647
1972	$948,647	18.74%	-$100,000	$159,023	$1,007,670
1973	$1,007,670	-14.42%	-$100,000	-$130,864	$776,805
1974	$776,805	-25.95%	*WIM*	-$201,547	$575,258
1975	$575,258	36.90%	*WIM*	$212,282	$787,540
1976	$787,540	23.72%	-$100,000	$163,061	$850,600
1977	$850,600	-7.03%	-$100,000	-$52,736	$697,864
1978	$697,864	6.59%	*WIM*	$46,011	$743,875
1979	$743,875	18.53%	-$100,000	$119,315	$763,190
1980	$763,190	31.65%	-$100,000	$209,881	$873,072
1981	$873,072	-4.64%	-$100,000	-$35,875	$737,197
1982	$737,197	20.38%	-$100,000	$129,831	$767,028
1983	$767,028	22.33%	-$100,000	$148,971	$816,000
1984	$816,000	6.08%	-$100,000	$43,543	$759,542

Year	Beg. Of Year Acct. Value	Earnings Rate	Spending Per Year	Growth	End of Year Acct. Value
1985	$759,542	31.16%	-$100,000	$205,506	$865,048
1986	$865,048	18.59%	-$100,000	$142,197	$907,245
1987	$907,245	5.78%	-$100,000	$46,669	$853,914
1988	$853,914	16.54%	-$100,000	$124,732	$878,646
1989	$878,646	31.44%	-$100,000	$244,792	$1,023,438
1990	$1,023,438	-3.07%	-$100,000	-$28,325	$895,113
1991	$895,113	29.98%	-$100,000	$238,392	$1,033,504
1992	$1,033,504	7.48%	-$100,000	$69,852	$1,003,357
1993	$1,003,357	9.98%	-$100,000	$90,126	$993,483
1994	$993,483	1.32%	-$100,000	$11,761	$905,244
1995	$905,244	37.20%	-$100,000	$299,518	$1,104,763
1996	$1,104,763	22.70%	-$100,000	$228,039	$1,232,801
1997	$1,232,801	33.12%	-$100,000	$375,179	$1,507,980
1998	$1,507,980	28.38%	-$100,000	$399,617	$1,807,597
1999	$1,807,597	20.87%	-$100,000	$356,426	$2,064,023

That's because you used an uncorrelated asset—a loan against your insurance policy—and you didn't take money out in a down market. During the years 1974, 1975, and 1978, you were able to adjust.

With the volatility buffer in place, you can take out almost twice what the Monte Carlo or interest methods will allow you to access, and you can still sleep well. (And indoors!) That's how important the economic power of uncorrelated assets can be.

2. Spend Assets Differently—Actuarial Science

With this strategy, you need to forget about the cash value of the WIM account and only focus on the death benefit. Remember that thing that came with the cash value that you were not really interested in when you first deposited money into this? Well now in retirement, that death benefit, or actuarial science, will supercharge your retirement income.

I call having a permanent death benefit, which is part of the high-cash-value life insurance, a "permission slip to spend."

Let me explain.

Abel and Baker are brothers. Each has saved $1 million. Abel had term insurance that expired at age sixty-five. He lives off the interest of his million, which is 4 percent a year. In a 35 percent tax bracket, he nets $26,000 per year. Here's what allows him to sleep at night: he knows if he dies at age eighty, there will still be $1 million left, which will go to his family. Over twenty years of retirement, Abel and his spouse will be able to spend $26,000 a year, or $520,000 total.

Permission Slip to Spend Assets Differently — Abel and Baker

Abel

Age	Gross Withdrawals Is EOY	Account Value	Earnings Rate	Annual Tax	Net Income	Legacy Value
65	$40,000	$1,000,000	4.00%	-$14,000	$26,000	$1,000,000
66	$40,000	$1,000,000	4.00%	-$14,000	$26,000	$1,000,000
67	$40,000	$1,000,000	4.00%	-$14,000	$26,000	$1,000,000
68	$40,000	$1,000,000	4.00%	-$14,000	$26,000	$1,000,000
69	$40,000	$1,000,000	4.00%	-$14,000	$26,000	$1,000,000
70	$40,000	$1,000,000	4.00%	-$14,000	$26,000	$1,000,000
71	$40,000	$1,000,000	4.00%	-$14,000	$26,000	$1,000,000
72	$40,000	$1,000,000	4.00%	-$14,000	$26,000	$1,000,000
73	$40,000	$1,000,000	4.00%	-$14,000	$26,000	$1,000,000
74	$40,000	$1,000,000	4.00%	-$14,000	$26,000	$1,000,000
75	$40,000	$1,000,000	4.00%	-$14,000	$26,000	$1,000,000
76	$40,000	$1,000,000	4.00%	-$14,000	$26,000	$1,000,000
77	$40,000	$1,000,000	4.00%	-$14,000	$26,000	$1,000,000
78	$40,000	$1,000,000	4.00%	-$14,000	$26,000	$1,000,000
79	$40,000	$1,000,000	4.00%	-$14,000	$26,000	$1,000,000
80	*$40,000*	*$1,000,000*	*4.00%*	*-$14,000*	*$26,000*	*$1,000,000*
81	$40,000	$1,000,000	4.00%	-$14,000	$26,000	$1,000,000
82	$40,000	$1,000,000	4.00%	-$14,000	$26,000	$1,000,000
83	$40,000	$1,000,000	4.00%	-$14,000	$26,000	$1,000,000
84	$40,000	$1,000,000	4.00%	-$14,000	$26,000	$1,000,000
Totals	*$800,000*	*$1,000,000*	*4.00%*	*-$280,000*	*$520,000*	*$1,000,000*

Baker

Age	Gross Withdrawals Is EOY	Account Value	Earnings Rate	Annual Tax	Net Income	Legacy Value
65	$73,582	$966,418	4.00%	-$14,000	$59,582	$1,966,418
66	$73,582	$931,493	4.00%	-$13,530	$60,052	$1,931,493
67	$73,582	$895,171	4.00%	-$13,041	$60,541	$1,895,171
68	$73,582	$857,396	4.00%	-$12,532	$61,049	$1,857,396
69	$73,582	$818,110	4.00%	-$12,004	$61,578	$1,818,110
70	$73,582	$777,253	4.00%	-$11,454	$62,128	$1,777,253
71	$73,582	$734,761	4.00%	-$10,882	$62,700	$1,734,761
72	$73,582	$690,570	4.00%	-$10,287	$63,295	$1,690,570
73	$73,582	$644,611	4.00%	-$9,668	$63,914	$1,644,611
74	$73,582	$596,814	4.00%	-$9,025	$64,557	$1,596,814
75	$73,582	$547,105	4.00%	-$8,355	$65,226	$1,547,105
76	$73,582	$495,407	4.00%	-$7,659	$65,922	$1,495,407
77	$73,582	$441,642	4.00%	-$6,936	$66,646	$1,441,642
78	$73,582	$385,726	4.00%	-$6,183	$67,399	$1,385,726
79	$73,582	$327,573	4.00%	-$5,400	$68,182	$1,327,573
80	*$73,582*	*$267,094*	*4.00%*	*-$4,586*	*$68,996*	*$1,267,094*
81	$73,582	$204,196	4.00%	-$3,739	$69,842	$1,204,196
82	$73,582	$138,782	4.00%	-$2,859	$70,723	$1,138,782
83	$73,582	$70,752	4.00%	-$1,943	$71,639	$1,070,752
84	$73,582	0	4.00%	-$991	$72,591	$1,000,000
Totals	*$1,471,635*	*$0*	*4.00%*	*-$165,072*	*$1,306,563*	*$1,000,000*

Baker, who also saved $1 million, happens to have $1 million of life insurance as well—because years ago, he bought a high-cash-value life insurance policy, and a death benefit came along with it. That $1 million death benefit is Baker's "permission slip" to spend his money differently. He can spend not only the same 4 percent interest that his brother is spending, but he can also spend down money from his principal, because the death benefit will make up the difference. If Baker dies at age 80, his account balance on his investment account will be only $267,094, but he has a $1 million death benefit, so his spouse will be protected.

Abel is able to spend over $65,000 after taxes per year because of his permission slip. Remember the retirement risk inflation? Look at Baker's after-tax income. It actually increases each year and keeps pace with inflation. Why? Look at his annual tax bill. It actually goes down each year because his account balance is going down each year—less money invested, less taxable earnings, and therefore less annual tax.

Baker and his spouse were able to spend $1,306,000 over twenty years of retirement versus his brother's $520,000. That is 2.5 times more spending!

That is the difference between a "just getting by" retirement and a "living the life" retirement.

We addressed the inflation risk, but what about some of the other retirement risks?

What if interest rates are low—like today, around 2 percent? Remember, with typical financial planning—the kind Abel is using—all the pressure is on the rate of return. If we change the interest rate from 4 percent to 2 percent, look at what happens to Abel's income.

It's cut in half—$13,000 per year, or $260,000 over twenty years, because all the pressure was on the rate of return. Baker has actuarial science (a death benefit) working for him.

If his interest rate drops to 2 percent, look at the net effect on his annual income. It ranges from $55,000 to $60,000, still increases each year, and pays Baker a total of $1.145 million over twenty years, instead of Abel's $260,000—almost 4.5 times as much.

Abel

Age	Gross Withdrawals Is EOY	Account Value	Earnings Rate	Annual Tax	Net Income	Legacy Value
65	$20,000	$1,000,000	2.00%	-$7,000	$13,000	$1,000,000
66	$20,000	$1,000,000	2.00%	-$7,000	$13,000	$1,000,000
67	$20,000	$1,000,000	2.00%	-$7,000	$13,000	$1,000,000
68	$20,000	$1,000,000	2.00%	-$7,000	$13,000	$1,000,000
69	$20,000	$1,000,000	2.00%	-$7,000	$13,000	$1,000,000
70	$20,000	$1,000,000	2.00%	-$7,000	$13,000	$1,000,000
71	$20,000	$1,000,000	2.00%	-$7,000	$13,000	$1,000,000
72	$20,000	$1,000,000	2.00%	-$7,000	$13,000	$1,000,000
73	$20,000	$1,000,000	2.00%	-$7,000	$13,000	$1,000,000
74	$20,000	$1,000,000	2.00%	-$7,000	$13,000	$1,000,000
75	$20,000	$1,000,000	2.00%	-$7,000	$13,000	$1,000,000
76	$20,000	$1,000,000	2.00%	-$7,000	$13,000	$1,000,000
77	$20,000	$1,000,000	2.00%	-$7,000	$13,000	$1,000,000
78	$20,000	$1,000,000	2.00%	-$7,000	$13,000	$1,000,000
79	$20,000	$1,000,000	2.00%	-$7,000	$13,000	$1,000,000
80	$20,000	$1,000,000	2.00%	-$7,000	$13,000	$1,000,000
81	$20,000	$1,000,000	2.00%	-$7,000	$13,000	$1,000,000
82	$20,000	$1,000,000	2.00%	-$7,000	$13,000	$1,000,000
83	$20,000	$1,000,000	2.00%	-$7,000	$13,000	$1,000,000
84	$20,000	$1,000,000	2.00%	-$7,000	$13,000	$1,000,000
Totals	*$400,000*	*$1,000,000*	*2.00%*	*-$140,000*	*$260,000*	*$1,000,000*

Baker

Age	Gross Withdrawals Is EOY	Account Value	Earnings Rate	Annual Tax	Net Income	Legacy Value
65	$61,157	$958,843	2.00%	-$7,000	$54,157	$1,958,943
66	$61,157	$916,863	2.00%	-$6,712	$54,445	$1,926,863
67	$61,157	$874,044	2.00%	-$6,418	$54,739	$1,874,044
68	$61,157	$830,368	2.00%	-$6,118	$55,038	$1,830,368
69	$61,157	$785,819	2.00%	-$5,813	$55,344	$1,785,819
70	$61,157	$740,378	2.00%	-$5,501	$55,656	$1,740,378
71	$61,157	$694,029	2.00%	-$5,183	$55,974	$1,694,029
72	$61,157	$646,753	2.00%	-$4,858	$56,299	$1,646,753
73	$61,157	$598,532	2.00%	-$4,527	$56,629	$1,598,532
74	$61,157	$549,345	2.00%	-$4,190	$56,967	$1,549,345
75	$61,157	$499,176	2.00%	-$3,845	$57,311	$1,499,176
76	$61,157	$448,002	2.00%	-$3,494	$57,662	$1,448,002
77	$61,157	$395,806	2.00%	-$3,136	$58,021	$1,395,806
78	$61,157	$342,565	2.00%	-$2,771	$58,386	$1,342,565
79	$61,157	$288,260	2.00%	-$2,398	$58,759	$12,288,260
80	$61,157	$232,868	2.00%	-$2,018	$59,139	$1,232,868
81	$61,157	$179,369	2.00%	-$1,630	$59,527	$1,176,369
82	$61,157	$118,739	2.00%	-$1,235	$59,922	$1,118,739
83	$61,157	$59,958	2.00%	-$831	$60,326	$1,059,958
84	$61,157	0	2.00%	-$420	$60,737	$1,000,000
Totals	*$1,223,134*	*$0*	*2.00%*	*-$78,097*	*$1,145,037*	*$1,000,000*

Let's look at just one more retirement risk: taxes. If (when) taxes are higher in retirement, how does that affect the brothers? If we assume they are both in a 50 percent tax bracket, Abel's income drops to $20,000 after tax, for a total of $400,000 over twenty years. Baker's income hardly drops at all. His twenty-year income was $1.3 million. At a 50 percent tax rate, it drops to $1.235 million. Not a big drop at all.

He has tamed many of the retirement risks.

Abel

Age	Gross Withdrawals Is EOY	Account Value	Earnings Rate	Annual Tax	Net Income	Legacy Value
65	$40,000	$1,000,000	4.00%	-$20,000	$20,000	$1,000,000
66	$40,000	$1,000,000	4.00%	-$20,000	$20,000	$1,000,000
67	$40,000	$1,000,000	4.00%	-$20,000	$20,000	$1,000,000
68	$40,000	$1,000,000	4.00%	-$20,000	$20,000	$1,000,000
69	$40,000	$1,000,000	4.00%	-$20,000	$20,000	$1,000,000
70	$40,000	$1,000,000	4.00%	-$20,000	$20,000	$1,000,000
71	$40,000	$1,000,000	4.00%	-$20,000	$20,000	$1,000,000
72	$40,000	$1,000,000	4.00%	-$20,000	$20,000	$1,000,000
73	$40,000	$1,000,000	4.00%	-$20,000	$20,000	$1,000,000
74	$40,000	$1,000,000	4.00%	-$20,000	$20,000	$1,000,000
75	$40,000	$1,000,000	4.00%	-$20,000	$20,000	$1,000,000
76	$40,000	$1,000,000	4.00%	-$20,000	$20,000	$1,000,000
77	$40,000	$1,000,000	4.00%	-$20,000	$20,000	$1,000,000
78	$40,000	$1,000,000	4.00%	-$20,000	$20,000	$1,000,000
79	$40,000	$1,000,000	4.00%	-$20,000	$20,000	$1,000,000
80	$40,000	$1,000,000	4.00%	-$20,000	$20,000	$1,000,000
81	$40,000	$1,000,000	4.00%	-$20,000	$20,000	$1,000,000
82	$40,000	$1,000,000	4.00%	-$20,000	$20,000	$1,000,000
83	$40,000	$1,000,000	4.00%	-$20,000	$20,000	$1,000,000
84	$40,000	$1,000,000	4.00%	-$20,000	$20,000	$1,000,000
Totals	*$800,000*	*$1,000,000*	*4.00%*	*-$400,000*	*$400,000*	*$1,000,000*

Baker

Age	Gross Withdrawals Is EOY	Account Value	Earnings Rate	Annual Tax	Net Income	Legacy Value
65	$73,582	$966,418	4.00%	-$20,000	$53,582	$1,966,418
66	$73,582	$931,493	4.00%	-$19,328	$54,253	$1,931,493
67	$73,582	$895,171	4.00%	-$18,630	$54,952	$1,895,171
68	$73,582	$857,396	4.00%	-$17,903	$55,678	$1,857,369
69	$73,582	$818,110	4.00%	-$17,148	$56,434	$1,818,110
70	$73,582	$777,253	4.00%	-$16,362	$57,220	$1,777,253
71	$73,582	$734,761	4.00%	-$15,545	$58,037	$1,734,761
72	$73,582	$690,570	4.00%	-$14,695	$58,887	$1,690,570
73	$73,582	$644,611	4.00%	-$13,811	$59,770	$1,644,611
74	$73,582	$596,814	4.00%	-$12,892	$60,690	$1,596,814
75	$73,582	$547,105	4.00%	-$11,936	$61,645	$1,547,105
76	$73,582	$495,407	4.00%	-$10,942	$62,640	$1,495,407
77	$73,582	$441,642	4.00%	-$9,908	$63,674	$1,441,642
78	$73,582	$385,726	4.00%	-$8,833	$64,749	$1,385,726
79	$73,582	$327,573	4.00%	-$7,715	$65,867	$1,327,573
80	$73,582	$267,094	4.00%	-$6,551	$67,030	$1,267,094
81	$73,582	$204,196	4.00%	-$5,342	$68,240	$1,204,196
82	$73,582	$138,782	4.00%	-$4,084	$69,498	$1,138,782
83	$73,582	$70,752	4.00%	-$2,776	$70,806	$1,070,752
84	$73,582	0	4.00%	-$1,415	$72,167	$1,000,000
Totals	***$1,471,635***	***$0***	***4.00%***	***-$235,818***	***$1,235,818***	***$1,000,000***

Now if you go back and look at the first Abel and Baker income projection, there is one thing you have to be aware of. At age eighty-five, Baker and his wife set up a virtual meeting with me to talk about their incredible retirement. By having a WIM account with a cash value *and* a permanent death benefit, they spent 2.5 to 3 times more money than they would have been able to otherwise (like Abel).

They were able to take their dream trip to New Zealand and Australia for two months. They saw all their grandchildren's special occasions, graduations, and birthdays. They spent winters in the South. And they never, ever worried about the markets, interest rates, or taxes, like Baker's brother did. Baker's wife went on to say it was probably this stress-free retirement that was their reason for the meeting today. They were both still in great health, and they had spent the $1 million of savings they had.

Baker's wife blurted out, "Baker didn't die!"

So the death benefit hadn't been paid yet. After we all chuckled, I assured her that we'd made plans for this.

3. Asset Insurance— What Other Assets Do You Have?

When you are working, what does a death benefit, or life insurance death benefit, insure? Well, it insures you. You are the one producing the income. If you don't come home, the death benefit is meant to replace the income you would have generated for the next ten to thirty years, depending on your age.

But in retirement, are you still producing an income? No. Your assets are producing the income. I like to think of life insurance as *asset insurance* in retirement.

Now before you think I created a new product, relax, life insurance doesn't change in retirement; it is still life insurance that will pay a death benefit when you die. I just want you to *think* about it differently. In the Abel and Baker scenario, Baker was using a "paydown" strategy. That is, he was paying down the $1 million of assets over a twenty-year period, with the idea if he dies at year ten or eighteen, for example, the death benefit would "replenish" those assets, and his spouse would be financially secure.

So if you have spent that asset ($1 million in savings), the question is, what other assets do you have that you could also use this "asset insurance" for?

Let's assume Baker and his wife have a house (or income property) valued at $1 million by the time they are eighty-five years old. Most eighty-five-year-olds would never dream of borrowing against their house at that age and leaving debt when they die. But if you have $1 million or $2 million of death benefit, why not?

Baker takes a $70,000 line of credit tax-free against his house from eighty-five until his death at age ninety. He and his wife maintain their lifestyle, and now he leaves a $1 million or more death benefit at age ninety. The loan and interest are paid off, and his wife has $600,000 in cash and a million-dollar-plus home.

Now, this is just one idea for additional assets. A much easier one is the WIM account. If Baker has the death benefit because of a WIM account, then two significant things have happened since he turned sixty-five. His death benefit *and* his cash value have grown significantly in those twenty years. He was at that point in the compound curve where the gains are huge (the side B that rich people hit). So the easier solution is to just start spending cash inside the policy—more on that in number 5.

4. Guaranteed Lifetime Income

An annuity is something not a lot of people think about before, or even in, retirement. Think of an annuity like a government worker's pension plan. They have a lifetime pension coming in every month until the day they die—guaranteed. That is what an annuity is. You trade assets or investments for a lifetime income, with certain guarantees. Even at today's low interest rates, a seventy-year-old can purchase a lifetime annuity of around 7 percent or more per year, with a ten-year guarantee period.

What does that mean? You give a financial institution $1 million at age seventy because you are tired of the markets, investing, etc., and they will pay you $70,000 per year until the day you die. That's double what the Monte Carlo method would pay. Still alive at age 110? Yep, you still get paid every year.

Remember the biggest retirement risk we will ever face, the one that made all the other retirement risks more likely to happen multiple times? Longevity. You have eliminated the biggest retirement risk of all. No matter how long you live, you will get paid. You'll double your income and reduce your biggest retirement risk.

What happens if you die one month after buying an annuity? The ten-year-guarantee period kicks in, and your beneficiary gets $70,000 per year for the remaining ten-year period. What if you die ten years and a day after buying the annuity? Zilch, zip, nada. There is nothing left for your spouse.

Now we know why most people can never buy an annuity if they have a spouse or other family members. They would leave their loved one(s) with nothing.

Fortunately, if you have a WIM account, you have options. Every WIM account has a death benefit. If you die at age eighty plus a day, there may not be any annuity payments left, but your spouse will receive a big, fat tax-free cheque from the insurance company. It will be a large death benefit because it compounded until you were eighty.

Now, I am not suggesting you go out and buy an annuity with all of your money. The purpose was to show you how many more options you will have in retirement with proper planning while you are saving for retirement. Many people will buy a small annuity to supplement government benefits and pensions to bring them up to a certain income so they know with certainty that they will always have at least *that* income for life. They spend their other money more sporadically.

One last note on annuities: if interest rates are up, so are annuity rates. I took over a client from a retired advisor. This client bought a lifetime annuity in the 1980s with a guaranteed payout for life that was around 15 percent, and she lived to be ninety-seven years old. Who knows what interest rates or annuity rates will be when you retire, but it would be nice to have the option.

5. Spend WIM Account Cash Values as Tax-Free Distributions

Similar to the corporate scenario, this is just a preview of what you can do. There are lots of details that need to be fully explained by an expert advisor.

One of the easiest-to-understand methods of spending your money more efficiently in retirement is to borrow against your cash value, and never pay the loan back. You would set up a bank loan and take tax-free loans against the WIM account. You would not make payments on the loan, and you would not make any interest payments. The loan and interest would be paid off with the death benefit after your death.

What is really interesting about this strategy is that you are still compounding interest until the day you die. You never cash out your policy or sell a portion of it; it keeps compounding at those really big late gains for life.

Most people save, and then start depleting their savings in retirement, which results in less and less growth per year because their investment balance is smaller. With the WIM strategy, you are the opposite. Your money continues to move along the compound interest curve, and you get even larger gains in retirement! You are on side B like the wealthy because now you *are* the wealthy.

With this strategy of spending money, four things will happen:

1. Every dollar you put into your WIM account through the years will come back to you with friends. For every dollar you put in, you and your family will get $3, $4, $5, $6, $7, or $8 back tax-free, depending upon your situation and when you started your WIM account.

2. You will have a lot more money to spend than the people who did not choose this strategy. However, it will not show up as taxable income. It will not affect your government benefits. You will not even get a tax slip for the income. It will be tax-free.

3. You will leave a legacy. There will always be some life insurance over and above the loan to leave as a legacy. You can plan to spend most of it while you're alive, but if something happens along the way, and you don't reach eighty-five or ninety, your loved ones will get a tax-free lump sum.

4. You will have a happier and less-stressed retirement as a result of your having eliminated financial worries.

These are just five of the many ways to spend money more efficiently in retirement; there are lots more. The goal of this chapter is to get you thinking about what you want in retirement. There are many options to spend significantly more in retirement and be able to adjust to whatever the actual realities are when you retire (interest rates, inflation, taxes, health, etc.)

or be stuck with the typical way—hoping the casino of Wall Street works out for you, with no plan B.

And now, let me ask you a question. Abel was worth a million dollars when he retired. Isn't this the first time you've ever said, "I want to be a millionaire, just not *that* millionaire!"?

PART TWO WRAP-UP

Defeating the 10 Big Things

Remember those ten reasons the deck was stacked against you? Let's take a look at them again, with the knowledge that the perfect savings and wealth management account *does* exist.

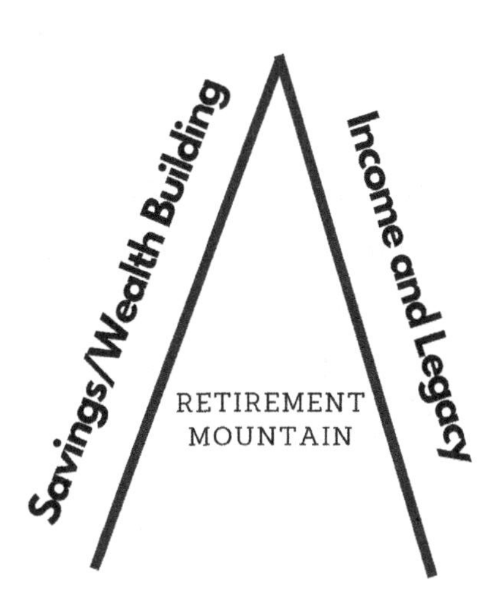

Phase 1—Savings and Wealth Building

1. No interrupted compounding. Guess what? With a WIM account, your compound interest is going to grow for your entire life.

2. *Or* asset instead of *and* asset. With a WIM account, your dollars are able to have multiple jobs at once. Your dollars are gaining interest, even while you're able to borrow against them for any number of things.

3. The four wealth destroyers. WIM accounts are able to mitigate or eliminate nearly all the wealth destroyers, including taxation.

4. No control (jail). Your WIM account puts you in control. You are the bank, and you're able to access your money when you need it, without telling anyone why.

5. Cannot use H.O.W. with current investments. The WIM account forms the foundation for the perfect Hierarchy of Wealth by giving you a bank that you're in control of to build that wealth.

6. Savings. With a WIM, you're able to put your money in a long-term investment vehicle without sacrificing your short-term liquidity.

7. No opportunity or emergency fund. At any time, you can access money using your WIM, no questions asked. You can pay it back whenever you want, or never.

Phase 2: Income and Legacy

8. Horrible investments to generate income. You're no longer relegated to interest or the Monte Carlo game. Instead, you'll be able to put your money to work making passive income, and even active income, whenever you want.

9. Pressure is on the rate of return. Instead of relying on a single economic power in retirement, you have four economic powers that can double your retirement income.

10. Retirement risks. A WIM protects you from a great deal of potential retirement risks, including potentially running out of money due to increased longevity.

By using the strategies of the wealthy, we have changed our financial lives. The middle-class roadblocks that were in place in Part One have been removed—clear sailing ahead.

We have achieved control over our money with unstructured loans and flexible deposits. We have created an *and* asset that will compound for the rest of our lives without that number one wealth destroyer—tax—strapped to our backs.

In fact, we have eliminated or reduced all four wealth destroyers. We are now able to take advantage of opportunities and deal with emergencies. We have access to the money we control, and we are able to invest in ourselves, our businesses, and real estate because our money is not in jail.

Even if we don't invest in real estate or business, our income in retirement is able to double while we enjoy a stress-free income with the middle-class retirement risks slayed because of our four economic powers.

And finally, if we don't live as long as we'd hoped, we have directed what would have gone to taxes all those years to our families—tax-free.

FINAL THOUGHTS

Should We Continue the Conversation?

F. Scott Fitzgerald is reputed to have said to Ernest Hemingway, "The rich are different from you and me," to which Hemingway replied, "Yes, they have more money!"

In this book, I've shared the main reason why wealthy people not only have more money than the middle class, but also keep making more money, day after day, month after month, year after year.

It all comes down to the fact that the wealthy put their money to work in multiple ways at the same time, just like banks, while middle-class people use their money for only one purpose at a time.

Wealthy people get the benefit of compounding their money forever, while middle-class people benefit from compound interest only for relatively short periods of time.

Wealthy people finance virtually everything they purchase without touching their own funds, which are left to compound and grow. Middle-class people, whether they're borrowers or savers, keep falling back to the zero line.

In short, wealthy people control their money, while middle-class people keep it locked up in "money jails," like RRSPs.

As a result, wealthy people can take advantage of sudden opportunities or pay for sudden crises without going into capital or otherwise damaging their financial positions. Too often, middle-class people can't take advantage of opportunities that come along—and worse, they are one crisis away from losing their homes or going broke.

Whom would you rather be?

We've also seen that banks are successful because they enjoy greater cash flow; higher velocity of money; and multiple uses of the same dollar, netting greater returns, than typical bank customers. Average people are subject to high fees when they use banking products. Middle-class people who put their money into mutual funds or pick individual stocks face enormous market risk, market volatility, high fees, and high taxes. And anyone thinking about the long term must consider the biggest risk of all—longevity risk, which, as we've seen, acts as a force multiplier on all the other risks people face.

What I've sought to do in these pages is to give you a strategy for "being the bank," for thinking and acting like wealthy people, instead of running the risks that typical middle-class people face—not just when they're ascending the mountain, but when they're coming down the other side.

If the ideas I've shared make sense, and I hope they do, then perhaps we should talk. It's been my privilege to serve business owners, real estate investors, and individuals out there in the working world who are doing the best they can to take care of their families and plan for the future.

As I learned a long time ago, and as I'm sure you suspect, the game is absolutely rigged in favor of the wealthy. The middle class doesn't stand a chance. Banks, investment companies, and the government see the middle class as a piggy bank from which fees and taxes can be extracted seemingly at will.

If you've had enough of being a pawn of these market and government forces, and you'd like to take control of your own financial future, I'd be honored to help you.

I like to think of real wealth as a snowball you just have to get moving down a hill. If you're interested, I can show you how, and together we can move you from the ranks of the middle class, which is a good place to be, to the ranks of the wealthy, which is where you really want to spend the rest of your life!

Do you want to get started? Ask your advisor if he or she has completed the authorized Infinite Banking Authorized Practitioner course. Ask your advisor how much of their own money they are putting into this (and if it's not a lot, they may not understand it). Even if your advisor can put a policy together correctly, there's almost a guarantee that something will eventually come up that you aren't expecting. That's where an expert comes in.

Do you want a pilot with three flights under his belt, or thousands, when something unexpected comes up while in the air?

I'm happy to have a no-obligation meeting with those who qualify.

My team and I are looking forward to hearing from you!

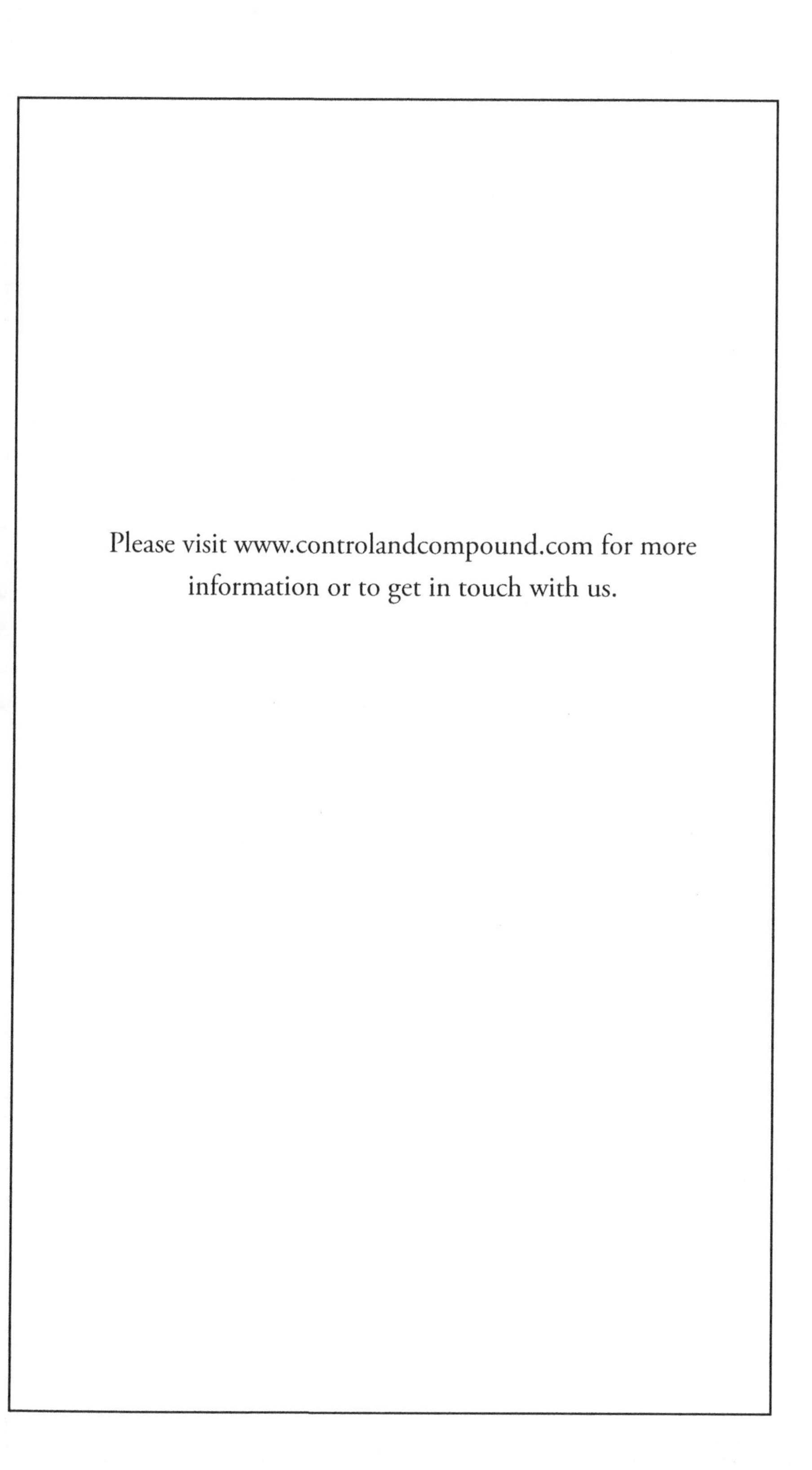

Please visit www.controlandcompound.com for more information or to get in touch with us.

Appendix

Chapter 3

Page 25:

The SPIVA Canada Scorecard provides a semiannual update on the active versus index debate in Canada. The SPIVA Canada Scorecard shows the performance of actively managed Canadian mutual funds compared with S&P Dow Jones Indices in their respective categories. For more information about the SPIVA Scorecard and the SPIVA methodology, visit www.spdji.com/spiva.